THE USA PATRIOT ACT

THE USA PATRIOT ACT

ALPHONSE B. EWING

Novinka Books
New York

Senior Editors: Susan Boriotti and Donna Dennis
Coordinating Editor: Tatiana Shohov
Office Manager: Annette Hellinger
Graphics: Wanda Serrano
Editorial Production: Vladimir Klestov, Matthew Kozlowski and Maya Columbus
Circulation: Ave Maria Gonzalez, Vera Popovic, Luis Aviles, Raymond Davis,
Melissa Diaz and Jeannie Pappas
Communications and Acquisitions: Serge P. Shohov
Marketing: Cathy DeGregory

Library of Congress Cataloging-in-Publication Data
Available Upon Request

ISBN: 1-59033-562-7.

An Imprint of Nova Science Publishers, Inc.
400 Oser Ave, Suite 1600
Hauppauge, New York 11788-3619
Tele. 631-231-7269 Fax 631-231-8175
e-mail: Novascience@earthlink.net
Web Site: http://www.novapublishers.com

Printed in the United States of America

CONTENTS

PREFACE

The USA Patriot Act passed in the wake of the September 11 terrorist attacks. It flows from a consultation draft circulated by the Department of Justice, to which Congress made substantial modifications and additions. The stated purpose of the Act is to enable law enforcement officials to track down and punish those responsible for the attacks and to protect against similar attacks.

The Act grants federal officials greater powers to trace and intercept terrorists' communications both for law enforcement and foreign intelligence purposes. It reinforces federal anti-money laundering laws and regulations in an effort to deny terrorists the resources necessary for future attacks. It tightens our immigration laws to close our borders to foreign terrorists and to expel those among us. Finally, it creates a few new federal crimes, such as the one outlawing terrorists' attacks on mass transit; increases the penalties for many others; and institutes several procedural changes, such as a longer statute of limitations for crimes of terrorism.

Critics have suggested that it may go too far. The authority to monitor e-mail traffic, to share grand jury information with intelligence and immigration officers, to confiscate property, and to impose new book-keeping requirements on financial institutions, are among the features troubling to some.

The Act itself responds to some of those reservations. Many of the wiretapping and foreign intelligence amendments sunset on December 31, 2005. The Act creates judicial safeguards for e-mail monitoring and grand jury disclosures; recognizes innocent owner defenses to forfeiture; and entrusts enhanced anti-money laundering powers to those regulatory authorities whose concerns include the well being of our financial institutions.

Chapter 1

THE USA PATRIOT ACT: A LEGAL ANALYSIS

Charles Doyle

SUMMARY

The USA PATRIOT Act passed in the wake of the September 11 terrorist attacks. It flows from a consultation draft circulated by the Department of Justice, to which Congress made substantial modifications and additions. The stated purpose of the Act is to enable law enforcement officials to track down and punish those responsible for the attacks and to protect against any similar attacks.

The Act grants federal officials greater powers to trace and intercept terrorists' communications both for law enforcement and foreign intelligence purposes. It re-enforces federal anti-money laundering laws and regulations in an effort to deny terrorists the resources necessary for future attacks. It tightens our immigration laws to close our borders to foreign terrorists and to expel those among us. Finally, it creates a few new federal crimes, such as the one outlawing terrorists' attacks on mass transit; increases the penalties for many others; and institutes several procedural changes, such as a longer statute of limitations for crimes of terrorism.

Critics have suggested that it may go too far. The authority to monitor e-mail traffic, to share grand jury information with intelligence and immigration officers, to confiscate property, and to impose new book-keeping requirements on financial institutions, are among the features troubling to some.

The Act itself responds to some of these reservations. Many of the wiretapping and foreign intelligence amendments sunset on December 31, 2005. The Act creates judicial safeguards for e-mail monitoring and grand jury disclosures; recognizes innocent owner defenses to forfeiture; and entrusts enhanced anti-money laundering powers to those regulatory authorities whose concerns include the well being of our financial institutions.

INTRODUCTION

Congress passed the USA PATRIOT Act (the Act) in response to the terrorists' attacks of September 11, 2001.[1] The Act gives federal officials greater authority to track and intercept communications, both for law enforcement and foreign intelligence gathering purposes. It vests the Secretary of the Treasury with regulatory powers to combat corruption of U.S. financial institutions for foreign money laundering purposes. It seeks to further close our borders to foreign terrorists and to detain and remove those within our borders. It creates new crimes, new penalties, and new procedural efficiencies for use against domestic and international terrorists. Although it is not without safeguards, critics contend some of its provisions go too far. Although it grants many of the enhancements sought by the Department of Justice, others are concerned that it does not go far enough.

The Act originated as H.R.2975 (the PATRIOT Act) in the House and S.1510 in the Senate (the USA Act).[2] S.1510 passed the Senate on October 11, 2001, 147 *Cong.Rec.* S10604 (daily ed.). The House Judiciary Committee reported out an amended version of H.R. 2975 on the same day, H.R.Rep.No. 107-236. The House passed H.R. 2975 the following day after substituting the text of H.R. 3108, 147 *Cong.Rec.* H6775-776 (daily ed. Oct. 12, 2001). The House-passed version incorporated most of the money laundering provisions found in an earlier House bill, H.R. 3004, many of

---

[1]P.L. 107-56, 115 Stat. 272 (2001); its full title is the "Uniting and Strengthening America by Providing Appropriate Tools Required to Intercept and Obstruct Terrorism (USA PATRIOT ACT)."

[2]H.R. 2975 was introduced by Representative Sensenbrenner for himself and Representatives Conyers, Hyde, Coble, Goodlatte, Jenkins, Jackson-Lee, Cannon, Meehan, Graham, Bachus, Wexler, Hostettler, Keller, Issa, Hart, Flake, Schiff, Thomas, Goss, Rangel, Berman and Lofgren; S.1510 by Senator Daschle for himself and Senators Lott, Leahy, Hatch, Graham, Shelby and Sarbanes.

which had counterparts in S.1510 as approved by the Senate.[3] The House subsequently passed a clean bill, H.R. 3162 (under suspension of the rules), which resolved the differences between H.R. 2975 and S.1510, 147 *Cong.Rec.* H7224 (daily ed. Oct. 24, 2001). The Senate agreed, 147 *Cong.Rec.* S10969 (daily ed. Oct. 24, 2001), and H.R. 3162 was sent to the President who signed it on October 26, 2001.

CRIMINAL INVESTIGATIONS: TRACKING AND GATHERING COMMUNICATIONS

A portion of the Act addresses issues suggested originally in a Department of Justice proposal circulated in mid-September.[4] The first of its suggestions called for amendments to federal surveillance laws, laws which govern the capture and tracking of suspected terrorists' communications within the United States. Federal law features a three tiered system, erected for the dual purpose of protecting the confidentiality of private telephone, face-to-face, and computer communications while enabling authorities to identify and intercept criminal communications.[5]

The tiers reflected the Supreme Court's interpretation of the Fourth Amendment's ban on unreasonable searches and seizures.[6] The Amendment protects private conversations, *Berger v. New York*, 388 U.S. 41 (1967); *Katz v. United States*, 389 U.S. 347 (1967). It does not cloak information, even highly personal information, for which there is no individual justifiable expectation of privacy, such as telephone company records of calls made to and from an individual's home, *Smith v. Maryland*, 442 U.S. 735 (1979), or

---

[3]H.R. 3004 was introduced by Representative Oxley for himself and Represenatives LaFalce, Leach, Maloney, Roukema, Bentsen, Hooley, Bereuter, Baker, Bachus, King, Kelly, Gillmore, Cantor, Riley, Latourette, Green (of Wisconsin), and Grucci; and reported out of the House Financial Services Committee with amendments on October 15, 2001, H.R.Rep.No. 107-250. H.R. 3004, as reported out, included Internet gambling amendments that were not included in H.R. 2975/H.R.3108.

[4]The Department's proposal, dated September 20, 2001, came with a brief section by section analysis. Both the proposal (*Draft*) and analysis (*DoJ*) were printed as an appendix in *Administration's Draft Anti-Terrorism Act of 2001, Hearing Before the House Comm. on the Judiciary*, 107th Cong., 1st Sess. 54 (2001).

[5]For a general discussion of federal law in the area prior to enactment of the Act, *see*, Stevens & Doyle, *Privacy: An Overview of Federal Statutes Governing Wiretappping and Electronic Eavesdropping*, CRS REP.NO. 98-327A (Aug. 8, 2001); Fishman & McKenna, WIRETAPPING AND EAVESDROPPING (2d ed. 1995 & 2001 Supp.).

[6]"The right of the people to be secure in their persons, houses, papers, and effects, against unreasonable searches and seizures, shall not be violated, and no Warrants shall issue, but

bank records of an individual's financial dealings, *United States v. Miller*, 425 U.S. 435 (1976).

Congress responded to *Berger* and *Katz*, with Title III of the Omnibus Crime Control and Safe Streets Act of 1968, 18 U.S.C. 2510-2522 (Title III). Title III, as amended, generally prohibits electronic eavesdropping on telephone conversations, face-to-face conversations, or computer and other forms of electronic communications, 18 U.S.C. 2511.[7] At the same time, it gives authorities a narrowly defined process for electronic surveillance to be used as a last resort in serious criminal cases. When approved by senior Justice Department officials,[8] law enforcement officers may seek a court order authorizing them to secretly capture conversations concerning any of a statutory list of offenses (predicate offenses), 18 U.S.C. 2516.[9]

---

upon probable cause, supported by Oath or affirmation, and particularly describing the place to be searched, and the persons or things to be seized," *U.S. Const.* Amend. IV.

[7]Although there are technical differences, the interception processes are popularly known as wiretapping, electronic eavesdropping, or electronic surveillance. The terms are used interchangeable here for purposes of convenience, but strictly speaking, wiretapping is limited to the mechanical or electronic interception of telephone conversations, while electronic eavesdropping or electronic surveillance refers to mechanical or electronic interception of communications generally.

[8]"The Attorney General, Deputy Attorney General, Associate Attorney General, or any Assistant Attorney General, any acting Assistant Attorney General, or any Deputy Assistant Attorney General or acting Deputy Assistant Attorney General in the Criminal Division specially designated by the Attorney General, may authorize an application to a Federal judge of competent jurisdiction for, and such judge may grant in conformity with section 2518 of this chapter an order authorizing or approving the interception of wire or oral communications by the Federal Bureau of Investigation, or a Federal agency having responsibility for the investigation of the offense as to which the application is made, when such interception may provide or has provided evidence of" one or more predicate offense, 18 U.S.C. 2516.

[9]The predicate offense list includes (a) felony violations of 42 U.S.C. 2274 through 2277 (enforcement of the Atomic Energy Act of 1954), 42 U.S.C. 2284 (sabotage of nuclear facilities or fuel), or of 18 U.S.C. ch. 37 (espionage), ch. 90 (protection of trade secrets), ch. 105 (sabotage), ch. 115 (treason), ch. 102 (riots), ch. 65 (malicious mischief), ch. 111 (destruction of vessels), or ch. 81 (piracy); (b) a violation of 29 U.S.C. 186 or 501(c) (restrictions on payments and loans to labor organizations), or any offense which involves murder, kidnapping, robbery, or extortion, and which is punishable under title 18 of the United States Code; (c) any offense which is punishable under 18 U.S.C. 201 (bribery of public officials and witnesses), 215 (bribery of bank officials), 224 (bribery in sporting contests), 844 (d), (e), (f), (g), (h), or (i) (unlawful use of explosives), 1032 (concealment of assets), 1084 (transmission of wagering information), 751 (escape), 1014 (loans and credit applications generally; renewals and discounts), 1503, 1512, and 1513 (influencing or injuring an officer, juror, or witness generally), 1510 (obstruction of criminal investigations), 1511 (obstruction of State or local law enforcement), 1751 (presidential and presidential staff assassination, kidnaping, or assault), 1951 (interference with commerce by threats or violence), 1952 (interstate and foreign travel or transportation in aid of racketeering enterprises), 1958 (use of interstate commerce facilities in the commission of murder for hire), 1959 (violent crimes in aid of racketeering activity), 1954 (offer, acceptance, or solicitation to influence operations of employee benefit plan), 1955 (prohibition of business

Title III court orders come replete with instructions describing the permissible duration and scope of the surveillance as well as the conversations which may be seized and the efforts to be taken to minimize the seizure of innocent conversations, 18 U.S.C. 2518. The court notifies the parties to any conversations seized under the order after the order expires, 18 U.S.C. 2518(8).

Below Title III, the next tier of privacy protection covers some of those matters which the Supreme Court has described as beyond the reach of the Fourth Amendment protection – telephone records, e-mail held in third party

---

enterprises of gambling), 1956 (laundering of monetary instruments), 1957 (engaging in monetary transactions in property derived from specified unlawful activity), 659 (theft from interstate shipment), 664 (embezzlement from pension and welfare funds), *1030 (computer abuse felonies)*, 1343 (fraud by wire, radio, or television), 1344 (bank fraud), 2251 and 2252 (sexual exploitation of children), 2312, 2313, 2314, and 2315 (interstate transportation of stolen property), 2321 (trafficking in certain motor vehicles or motor vehicle parts), 1203 (hostage taking), 1029 (fraud and related activity in connection with access devices), 3146 (penalty for failure to appear), 3521(b)(3) (witness relocation and assistance), 32 (destruction of aircraft or aircraft facilities), 38 (aircraft parts fraud), 1963 (violations with respect to racketeer influenced and corrupt organizations), 115 (threatening or retaliating against a Federal official), 1341 (mail fraud), 351 (violations with respect to congressional, Cabinet, or Supreme Court assassinations, kidnaping, or assault), 831 (prohibited transactions involving nuclear materials), 33 (destruction of motor vehicles or motor vehicle facilities), 175 (biological weapons), 1992 (wrecking trains), a felony violation of 1028 (production of false identification documentation), 1425 (procurement of citizenship or nationalization unlawfully), 1426 (reproduction of naturalization or citizenship papers), 1427 (sale of naturalization or citizenship papers), 1541 (passport issuance without authority), 1542 (false statements in passport applications), 1543 (forgery or false use of passports), 1544 (misuse of passports), or 1546 (fraud and misuse of visas, permits, and other documents); (d) any offense involving counterfeiting punishable under 18 U.S.C. 471, 472, or 473; (e) any offense involving fraud connected with a case under title 11 or the manufacture, importation, receiving, concealment, buying, selling, or otherwise dealing in narcotic drugs, marihuana, or other dangerous drugs, punishable under any law of the United States; (f) any offense including extortionate credit transactions under 18 U.S.C. 892, 893, or 894; (g) a violation of 31 U.S.C. 5322 (dealing with the reporting of currency transactions); (h) any felony violation of 18 U.S.C. 2511 and 2512 (interception and disclosure of certain communications and to certain intercepting devices); (i) any felony violation of 18 U.S.C. ch. 71 (obscenity); (j) 49 U.S.C. 60123(b) (destruction of a natural gas pipeline), 46502 (aircraft piracy); (k) 22 U.S.C. 2778 (Arms Export Control Act); (l) the location of any fugitive from justice from an offense described in this section; (m) a violation of 8 U.S.C. 1324, 1327, or 1328; (n) any felony violation of 18 U.S.C. 922, 924 (firearms); (o) any violation of 26 U.S.C. 5861 (firearms); (p) a felony violation of 18 U.S.C. 1028 (production of false identification documents), 1542 (false statements in passport applications), 1546 (fraud and misuse of visas, permits, and other documents) or a violation of 8 U.S.C. 1324, 1327, or 1328 (smuggling of aliens); *(p) 229 (chemical weapons), 2332 (terrorist violence against Americans overseas), 2332a (weapons of mass destruction), 2332b (multinational terrorism), 2332d (financial transactions with countries supporting terrorism), 2339A (support of terrorist), 2332B (support of terrorist organizations);* (r) any conspiracy to commit any of these, 18 U.S.C. 2516(1)(crimes added by the Act in italics). Other than telephone face to face conversations (*i.e.*, electronic communications), the approval of senior Justice Department officials is not required and an order may be sought in any felony investigation, 18 U.S.C. 2516(3).

storage, and the like, 18 U.S.C. 2701-2709 (Chapter 121). Here, the law permits law enforcement access, ordinarily pursuant to a warrant or court order or under a subpoena in some cases, but in connection with *any* criminal investigation and without the extraordinary levels of approval or constraint that mark a Title III interception, 18 U.S.C. 2703.

Least demanding and perhaps least intrusive of all is the procedure that governs court orders approving the government's use of trap and trace devices and pen registers, a kind of secret "caller id", which identify the source and destination of calls made to and from a particular telephone, 18 U.S.C. 3121-3127 (Chapter 206). The orders are available based on the government's certification, rather than a finding of the court, that the use of the device is likely to produce information relevant to the investigation of a crime, any crime, 18 U.S.C. 3123. The devices record no more than the identity of the participants in a telephone conversation,[10] but neither the orders nor the results they produce need ever be revealed to the participants.

The Act modifies the procedures at each of the three levels. It:

- permits pen register and trap and trace orders for electronic communications (*e.g.*, e-mail)
- authorizes nationwide execution of court orders for pen registers, trap and trace devices, and access to stored e-mail or communication records
- treats stored voice mail like stored e-mail (rather than like telephone conversations)
- permits authorities to intercept communications to and from a trespasser within a computer system (with the permission of the system's owner)
- adds terrorist and computer crimes to Title III's predicate offense list
- re-enforces protection for those who help execute Title III, ch. 121, and ch. 206 orders
- encourages cooperation between law enforcement and foreign intelligence investigators
- establishes a claim against the U.S. for certain communications privacy violations by government personnel

[10]Or more precisely, they reveal no more than the identity of the numbers assigned to the telephone lines activated for a particular communication.

- terminates the authority found in many of the these provisions and several of the foreign intelligence amendments with a sunset provision (Dec. 31, 2005).

Pen Registers and Trap and Trace Devices

In section 216, the Act allows court orders authorizing trap and trace devices and pen registers to be used to capture source and addressee information for computer conversations (*e.g.*, e-mail) as well as telephone conversations, 18 U.S.C. 3121, 3123. In answer to objections that e-mail header information can be more revealing than a telephone number, it creates a detailed report to the court, 18 U.S.C. 3123(a)(3).[11]

The use of pen registers or trap and trace devices was limited at one time to the judicial district in which the order was issued, 18 U.S.C. 3123 (2000 ed.). Under section 216, a court with jurisdiction over the crime under investigation may issue an order to be executed anywhere in the United States, 18 U.S.C. 3123(b)(1)(C), 3127(2).[12]

[11]"Where the law enforcement agency implementing an ex parte order under this subsection seeks to do so by installing and using its own pen register or trap and trace device on a packet-switched data network of a provider of electronic communication service to the public the agency shall ensure that a record will be maintained which will identify – (i) any officer or officers who installed the device and any officer or officers who accessed the device to obtain information from the network; (ii) the date and time the device was installed, the date and time the device was uninstalled, and the date, time, and duration of each time the device is accessed to obtain information; (iii) the configuration of the device at the time of its installation and any subsequent modification thereof; and (iv) any information which has been collected by the device. To the extent that the pen register or trap and trace device can be set automatically to record this information electronically, the record shall be maintained electronically throughout the installation and use of the such device.

"(B) The record maintained under subparagraph (A) shall be provided ex parte and under seal to the court which entered the ex parte order authorizing the installation and use of the device within 30 days after termination of the order (including any extensions thereof)," section 216(b)(1).

[12]The Justice Department urged the change in the name of expediency, "At present, the government must apply for new pen trap orders in every jurisdiction where an investigation is being pursued. Hence, law enforcement officers tracking a suspected terrorist in multiple jurisdictions must waste valuable time and resources by obtaining a duplicative order in each jurisdiction," *DoJ* at § 101. Here and throughout citations to the United States Code (U.S.C.) without reference to an edition refer to the current Code; references to the 2000 edition of the Code refer to the law prior to amendment by the Act.

Communications Records and Stored E-Mail

With respect to chapter 126, relating among other things to the content of stored e-mail and to communications records held by third parties, the law permits criminal investigators to retrieve the content of electronic communications in storage, like e-mail, with a search warrant, and if the communication has been in remote storage for more than 180 days without notifying the subscriber, 18 U.S.C. 2703(a),(b). A warrant will also suffice to seize records describing telephone and other communications transactions without customer notice, 18 U.S.C. 2703(c). In the absence of the probable cause necessary for a warrant but with a showing of reasonable grounds to believe that the information sought is relevant to a criminal investigation, officers are entitled to a court order mandating access to electronic communications in remote storage for more than 180 days or to communications records, 18 U.S.C. 2703(b),(c). They can obtain a limited amount of record information (subscribers names and addresses, telephone numbers, billing records and the like) using an administrative, grand jury, or trial court subpoena, 18 U.S.C. 2703(c)(1)(C). There is no subscriber notification in record cases. Elsewhere, the court may delay customer notification in the face of exigent circumstances or if notice is likely to seriously jeopardize the investigation or unduly delay the trial, 18 U.S.C. 2705.

In order to streamline the investigation process, the Act, in section 210, adds credit card and bank account numbers to the information law enforcement officials may subpoena from a communications service provider's customer records, 18 U.S.C. 2703(c)(1)(C).[13]

Another streamlining amendment, section 220, eliminates the jurisdictional restrictions on access to the content of stored e-mail pursuant to a court order. Previously, only a federal court in the district in which the e-mail was stored could issue the order. Under section 220, federal courts in

[13]Prior to the amendment, "investigators [could] not use a subpoena to obtain such records as credit card number or other form of payment. In many cases, users register with Internet service providers using false names, making the form of payment critical to determining the user's true identity.... this information [could] only be obtained by the slower and more cumbersome process of a court order. In fast-moving investigation[s] such as terrorist bombings – in which Internet communications are a critical method of identifying conspirators and in determining the source of the attacks – the delay necessitated by the use of court orders can often be important. Obtaining billing and other information can identify not only the perpetrator but also give valuable information about the financial accounts of those responsible and their conspirators," *DoJ* at § 107.

the district where an offense under investigation occurred may issue orders applicable "without geographic limitation," 18 U.S.C. 2703.[14]

The Act, in section 209, treats voice mail like e-mail, that is, subject to the warrant or court order procedure, rather than to the more demanding coverage of Title III once required, *United States v. Smith*, 155 F.3d 1050, 1055-56 (9th Cir. 1998).

Finally, the Act resolves a conflict between chapter 121 and the federal law governing cable companies. Government entities may have access to cable company customer records only under a court order following an adversary hearing if they can show that the records will evidence that the customer is or has engaged in criminal activity, 47 U.S.C.511(h). When cable companies began offering telephone and other communications services the question arose whether the more demanding cable rules applied or whether law enforcement agencies were entitled to ex parte court orders under the no-notice procedures applicable to communications providers.[15] The Act makes it clear that the cable rules apply when cable television viewing services are involved and that the communications rules of chapter

[14]Speaking of the law before amendment, DoJ explained, "Current law requires the government to use a search warrant to compel a provider to disclose unopened e-mail. 18 U.S.C. §2703(a). Because Federal Rule of Criminal Procedure 41 requires that the 'property' to be obtained 'be within the district' of the issuing court, however, the rule may not allow the issuance of §2703(a) warrants for e-mail located in other districts. Thus, for example, where an investigator in Boston is seeking electronic e-mail in the Yahoo! account of a suspected terrorist, he may need to coordinate with agents, prosecutors, and judges in the Northern District of California, none of whom have any other involvement in the investigation. This electronic communications information can be critical in establishing relationships, motives, means, and plans of terrorists. Moreover, it is equally relevant to cyber-incidents in which a terrorist motive has not (but may well be) identified. Finally, even cases that require the quickest response (kidnappings, threats, or other dangers to public safety or the economy) may rest on evidence gathered under §2703(a). To further public safety, this section accordingly authorizes courts with jurisdiction over investigations to compel evidence directly, without requiring the intervention of their counterparts in other districts where major Internet service providers are located," *DoJ* at §108.

[15]*See e.g., DoJ* at §109 ("Law enforcement must have the capability to trace, intercept, and obtain records of the communications of terrorists and other criminals with great speed, even if they choose to use a cable provider for their telephone and Internet service. This section amends the Cable Communications Policy Act ('Cable Act') to clarify that when a cable company acts as a telephone company or an Internet service provider, it must comply with the same laws governing the interception and disclosure of wire and electronic communications that apply to any other telephone company or Internet service provider. The Cable Act, passed in 1984 to regulate various aspects of the cable television industry, could not take into account the changes in technology that have occurred over the last seventeen years. Cable television companies now often provide Internet access and telephone service in addition to television programming. Because of perceived conflicts between the Cable Act and laws that govern law enforcement's access to communications and records of communications carried by cable companies, cable providers have refused to comply with lawful court orders, thereby slowing or ending critical investigations").

121 apply when a cable company or anyone else provides communications services, section 211.

Electronic Surveillance

To Title III's predicate offense list, the Act adds cybercrime (18 U.S.C. 1030) and several terrorists crimes, sections 201, 202.[16] A second cybercrime initiative, section 217, permits law enforcement officials to intercept the communications of an intruder within a protected computer system (*i.e.*, a system used by the federal government, a financial institution, or one used in interstate or foreign commerce or communication), without the necessity of a warrant or court order, 18 U.S.C. 2511(2)(*i*). Yet only the interloper's intruding communications, those to or from the invaded system, are exposed under the section. The Justice Department originally sought the change because the law then did not clearly allow victims of computer trespassing to request law enforcement assistance in monitoring unauthorized attacks as they occur.[17]

Criminal Investigators' Access to Foreign Intelligence Information

The Act clearly contemplates closer working relations between criminal investigators and foreign intelligence investigators, particular in cases of international terrorism.[18] It amends the Foreign Intelligence Surveillance Act (FISA) to that end. As originally enacted, the application for a surveillance order under FISA required certification of the fact that "*the* purpose for the

---

[16] 18 U.S.C. 229 (chemical weapons), 2332(terrorist acts of violence committed against Americans overseas), 2332a(use of weapons of mass destruction), 2332b(acts of terrorism transcending national boundaries), 2332d(financial transactions with countries which support terrorists), 2339A(providing material support to terrorists), and 2339B(providing material support to terrorist organizations).

[17] "Because service providers often lack the expertise, equipment, or financial resources required to monitor attacks themselves as permitted under current law, they often have no way to exercise their rights to protect themselves from unauthorized attackers. Moreover, such attackers can target critical infrastructures and engage in cyberterrorism," *DoJ* at §106. Elsewhere the Act defines "electronic surveillance" for purposes of the Foreign Intelligence Surveillance Act (FISA) to emphasize that the law enforcement authority for this intruder surveillance does not confer similar authority for purposes of foreign intelligence gathering, section 1003 (50 U.S.C. 1801(f)(2)).

surveillance is to obtain foreign intelligence information," 50 U.S.C. 1804(a)(7)(B)(2000 ed.) (emphasis added), although it anticipated that any evidence divulged as a result might be turned over to law enforcement officials. Defendants often questioned whether authorities had used a FISA surveillance order against them in order to avoid the predicate crime threshold for a Title III order. Out of these challenges arose the notion that perhaps "the purpose" might not always mean the sole purpose. The case law indicated that, while an expectation that evidence of a crime might be discovered did not preclude a FISA order, at such time as a criminal prosecution became the focus of the investigation officials were required to either end surveillance or secure an order under Title III.[19]

---

[18]For a general discussion of federal intelligence and law enforcement cooperation, *see*, Best, *Intelligence and Law Enforcement: Countering Transnational Threats to the U.S.*, CRS REP.NO. RL30252 (Dec. 3, 2001).

[19]Before FISA, several lower federal courts recognized a foreign intelligence exception to the Fourth Amendment's warrant clause. It is here that the "primary purpose" notion originated. In *United States v. Truong Dinh Hung*, 629 F.2d 908, 915 (4th Cir. 1980), decided after FISA on the basis of pre-existing law, the court declared, "as the district court ruled, the executive should be excused from securing a warrant only when the surveillance is conducted 'primarily' for foreign intelligence reasons. We think that the district court adopted the proper test, because once surveillance becomes primarily a criminal investigation, the courts are entirely competent to make the usual probable cause determination, and because, importantly, individual privacy interests come to the fore and government foreign policy concerns recede when the government is primarily attempting to form the basis for a criminal prosecution." Subsequent case law, however, is not as clear as it might be: *see e.g., United States v. Duggan*, 743 F.2d 59, 77 (2d Cir. 1984)("FISA permits federal officials to obtain orders authorizing electronic surveillance 'for the purpose of obtaining foreign intelligence information.' The requirement that foreign intelligence information be the primary objective of the surveillance is plain not only from the language of Sec. 1802(b) but also from the requirements in Sec. 1804 as to what the application must contain. The application must contain a certification by a designated official of the executive branch that the purpose of the surveillance is to acquire foreign intelligence information, and the certification must set forth the basis for the certifying officials's belief that the information sought is the type of foreign intelligence information described"); *United States v. Pelton*, 835 F.2d 1067, 1075-76 (4th Cir. 1987)("We also reject Pelton's claim that the 1985 FISA surveillance was conducted primarily for the purpose of his criminal prosecution, and not primarily for the purpose of obtaining foreign intelligence information.... We agree with the district court that the primary purpose of the surveillance, both initially and throughout was to gather foreign intelligence information. It is clear that otherwise valid FISA surveillance is not tainted simply because the government can anticipate that the fruits of the surveillance may later be used...as evidence in a criminal trial"); *United States v. Sarkissian*, 841 F.2d 959, 907-8 (9th Cir. 1988)("Defendants rely on the primary purpose test articulated in *United States v. Truong Dinh Hung*.... One other court has applied the primary purpose test. Another court has rejected it ... distinguishing *Truong*. A third court has declined to decide the issue. We also decline to decide the issue"); *United States v. Johnson*, 952 F.2d 565, 572 (1st Cir. 1991)("Appellants attack the government's surveillance on the ground that it was undertaken not for foreign intelligence purposes, but to gather evidence for a criminal prosecution. FISA applications must contain, among other things, a certification that the purpose of the requested surveillance is the gathering of foreign intelligence information....Although the evidence obtained under FISA subsequently may be

The Justice Department sought FISA surveillance and physical search authority on the basis of "a" foreign intelligence purpose.[20] Section 218 of the Act insists that foreign intelligence gathering be a "significant purpose" for the request for the FISA surveillance or physical search order, 50 U.S.C. 1804(a)(7)(B), 1823(a)(7)(B), a more demanding standard than the "a purpose" threshold proposed by the Justice Department, but a clear departure from the original "the purpose" entry point. FISA once described a singular foreign intelligence focus prerequisite for any FISA surveillance application. Section 504 of the Act further encourages coordination between intelligence and law enforcement officials, and states that such coordination is no impediment to a "significant purpose" certification, 50 U.S.C. 1806(k), 1825(k).[21]

Protective Measures

The Act re-enforces two kinds of safeguards, one set designed to prevent abuse and the other to protect those who assist the government. The sunset clause is perhaps the best known of the Act's safeguards. Under the direction of section 224, many of the law enforcement and foreign intelligence authorities granted by the Act expire as of December 31, 2005.[22] The Act

used in criminal prosecutions, the investigation of criminal activity cannot be the primary purpose of the surveillance").

[20] "Current law requires that FISA be used only where foreign intelligence gathering is the sole or primary purpose of the investigation. This section will clarify that the certification of a FISA request is supportable where foreign intelligence gathering is 'a' purpose of the investigation. This change would eliminate the current need continually to evaluate the relative weight of criminal and intelligence purposes, and would facilitate information sharing between law enforcement and foreign intelligence authorities which is critical to the success of anti-terrorism efforts," *DoJ* at §153.

[21] "(k)(1) Federal officers who conduct electronic surveillance to acquire foreign intelligence information under this title may consult with Federal law enforcement officers to coordinate efforts to investigate or protect against – (A) actual or potential attack or other grave hostile acts of a foreign power or an agent of a foreign power; (B) sabotage or international terrorism by a foreign power or an agent of a foreign power; or (C) clandestine intelligence activities by an intelligence service or network of a foreign power or by an agent of a foreign power. (2) Coordination authorized under paragraph (1) shall not preclude the certification required by section 104(a)(7)(B) or the entry of an order under section 105." FISA defines "foreign power" and "agent of a foreign power" broadly, *see* note 33, *infra*, quoting, 50 U.S.C. 1801.

[22] "(a) Except as provided in subsection (b), this title and the amendments made by this title (other than sections 203(a)[sharing grand jury information], 203(c)[procedures for sharing grand jury information], 205 [FBI translators], 208 [seizure of stored voice-mail], 210[subpoenas for communications provider customer records], 211 [access to cable company communication service records], 213[sneak and peek], 216[pen register and trap and trace device amendments], 221[trade sanctions], and 222[assistance to law enforcement],

also fills some of the gaps in earlier sanctions available for official, abusive invasions of privacy. Prior law made it a federal crime to violate Title III (wiretapping), chapter 121 (e-mail and communications records), or chapter 206 (pen registers and trap and trace devices).[23] Victims of offenses under Title III and chapter 121 (but not chapter 206) were entitled to damages (punitive damages in some cases) and reasonable attorneys' fees,[24] but could not recover against the United States.[25] Chapter 121 alone insisted upon an investigation into whether disciplinary action ought to be taken when federal officers or employees were found to have intentionally violated its proscriptions, 18 U.S.C. 2707.

The Act augments these sanctions by authorizing a claim against the United States for not less than $10,000 and costs for violations of Title III, chapter 121, or the Foreign Intelligence Surveillance Act (FISA), by federal officials, and emphasizing the prospect of administrative discipline for offending federal officials, section 223.

Finally, the Act instructs the Department of Justice's Inspector General to designate an official to receive and review complaints of civil liberties violations by DoJ officers and employees, section 1001.

The second category of protective measures applies to service providers and others who help authorities track and gather communications information. For example, section 815 immunizes service providers who in good faith preserve customer records at the government's request until a

---

and the amendments made by those sections) shall cease to have effect on December 31, 2005.

"(b) With respect to any particular foreign intelligence investigation that began before the date on which the provisions referred to in subsection (a) cease to have effect, or with respect to any particular offense or potential offense that began or occurred before the date on which such provisions cease to have effect, such provisions shall continue in effect," section 224.

The sections which expire are: 201 and 202 (adding certain terrorism crimes to the predicate list for Title III), 293(b)(sharing Title III information with foreign intelligence officers), 204 (clarifying the foreign intelligence exception to the law enforcement pen register and trap and trace device provisions), 206 (roving foreign intelligence surveillance), 207 (duration of foreign intelligence surveillance orders and extensions), 209 (treatment of voice mail as e-mail rather than as telephone conversation), 212 (service provider disclosures in emergency cases), 214 (authority for pen registers and trap and trace devices in foreign intelligence cases), 215 (production of tangible items in foreign intelligence investigations), 217 (intercepting computer trespassers communications), 218 (foreign intelligence surveillance when foreign intelligence gathering is "a significant" reason rather than "the" reason for the surveillance), 219 (nationwide terrorism search warrants), 220 (nationwide communication records and stored e-mail search warrants), 223 (civil liability and administrative discipline for violations of Title III, chapter 121, and certain foreign intelligence prohibitions), and 225 (immunity for foreign intelligence surveillance assistance).

[23] 18 U.S.C. 2511, 2701, and 3121 (2000 ed.), respectively.

[24] 18 U.S.C. 2520 and 2707 (2000 ed.).

court order authorizing access can be obtained.[26] Another allows providers to disclose customer records to protect the provider's rights and property and to disclose stored customer communications and records in emergency circumstances, section 212. Under pre-existing law providers could disclose the content of stored communications but not customer records. The Justice Department recommended the changes in the interests of greater protection against cybercrimes committed by terrorists and others.[27] A third section, section 222 promises reasonable compensation for service providers and anyone else who help law enforcement install or apply pen registers or trap and trace devices,[28] but makes it clear that nothing in the Act is intended to expand communications providers' obligation to make modifications in their systems in order to accommodate law enforcement needs.[29]

---

[25] *Spock v. United States*, 464 F.Supp. 510, 514 n.2 (S.D.N.Y. 1978); *Asmar v. IRS*, 680 F.Supp. 248, 250 (E.D.Mich. 1987).

[26] Prior law already granted service providers immunity for disclosure of customer records in compliance with a court access order, 18 U.S.C. 2703(f).

[27] "Existing law contains no provision that allows providers of electronic communications service to disclose the communications (or records relating to such communications) of their customers or subscribers in emergencies that threaten death or serious bodily injury. This section amends 18 U.S.C. §2702 to authorize such disclosures if the provider reasonably believes that an emergency involving immediate danger of death or serious physical injury to any person requires disclosure of the information without delay.

"Current law also contains an odd disconnect: a provider may disclose the *contents* of the customer's communications in order to protect its rights or property but the current statute does not expressly permit a provider to voluntarily disclose *non-content* records (such as a subscriber's login records). 18 U.S.C. 2702(b)(5). This problem substantially hinders the ability of providers to protect themselves from cyber-terrorists and criminals. Yet the right to disclose the contents of communications necessarily implies the less intrusive ability to disclose non-content records. In order to promote the protection of our nation's critical infrastructures, this section's amendments allow communications providers to voluntarily disclose both content and non-content records to protect their computer systems," *DoJ* at §110.

[28] Chapter 206 had long guaranteed providers and others reasonable compensation, 18 U.S.C. 3124(c), but section 216 of the Act expands the circumstances under which the authorities may request assistance including requests for the help of those not specifically mentioned in the court order. Section 222 makes it clear the expanded obligation to provide assistance is matched by a corresponding right to compensation.

[29] Thus in the name of assisting in the execution of Title III, chapter 121, or chapter 206 order, the courts may not cite the Act as the basis for an order compelling a service provider to make system modifications or provide any other technical assistance not already required under 18 U.S.C. 2518(4), 2706, or 3124(c), *see*, H.R.Rep.No. 107-236, at 62-3 (2001) (emphasis added) ("This Act is not intended to affect obligations under Communications Assistance for Law Enforcement Act [which addresses law enforcement-beneficial system modifications and the compensation to be paid for the changes], nor does the act impose any *additional* technical obligation or requirement on a provider of wire or electronic communication service or other person to furnish facilities or technical assistance").

FOREIGN INTELLIGENCE INVESTIGATIONS

Although both criminal investigations and foreign intelligence investigations are conducted in the United States, criminal investigations seek information about unlawful activity; foreign intelligence investigations seek information about other countries and their citizens. Foreign intelligence is not limited to criminal, hostile, or even governmental activity. Simply being foreign is enough.[30]

Restrictions on intelligence gathering within the United States mirror American abhorrence of the creation of a secret police, coupled with memories of intelligence gathering practices during the Vietnam conflict which some felt threatened to chill robust public debate. Yet there is no absolute ban on foreign intelligence gathering in the United States. Congress enacted the Foreign Intelligence Surveillance Act (FISA),[31] something of a Title III for foreign intelligence wiretapping conducted in this country, after the Supreme Court made it clear that the President's authority to see to national security was insufficient to excuse warrantless wiretapping of suspected terrorists who had no identifiable foreign connections, *United States v. United States District Court*, 407 U.S. 297 (1972). FISA later grew to include procedures for physical searches in foreign intelligence cases, 50 U.S.C. 1821-1829, for pen register and trap and trace orders, 50 U.S.C. 1841-1846, and for access to records from businesses engaged in car rentals, motel accommodations, and storage lockers, 50 U.S.C. 1861-1863 (2000 ed). Intelligence authorities gained narrow passages through other privacy barriers as well.[32]

In many instances, access was limited to information related to the activities of foreign governments or their agents in this country, not simply relating to something foreign here. FISA, for example, is directed at foreign governments, international terrorists, and their agents, spies and saboteurs.[33]

---

[30]*E.g.*, As amended by section 902 of the Act, "'foreign intelligence' means information relating to the capabilities, intentions, or activities of foreign governments or elements thereof, foreign organizations, or foreign persons, *or international terrorist activities*," 50 U.S.C. 401a(2)(language added by the Act in italics).

[31]50 U.S.C. 1801 *et seq.*

[32]*E.g.*, 18 U.S.C. 2709 (counterintelligence access to telephone toll and transaction records), 12 U.S.C. 3414 (right to financial privacy), 15 U.S.C. 1681u(fair credit reporting).

[33]"As used in this subchapter: (a) 'Foreign power' means – (1) a foreign government or any component thereof, whether or not recognized by the United States; (2) a faction of a foreign nation or nations, not substantially composed of United States persons; (3) an entity that is openly acknowledged by a foreign government or governments to be directed and controlled by such foreign government or governments; (4) a group engaged in international terrorism or activities in preparation therefor; (5) a foreign-based political organization, not

There were and still are extra safeguards if it appears that an intelligence investigation may generate information about Americans ("United States persons," *i.e.*, citizens or permanent resident aliens).[34] The procedures tend

substantially composed of United States persons; or (6) an entity that is directed and controlled by a foreign government or governments.

"(b) 'Agent of a foreign power' means – (1) any person other than a United States person, who – (A) acts in the United States as an officer or employee of a foreign power, or as a member of a foreign power as defined in subsection (a)(4) of this section; (B) acts for or on behalf of a foreign power which engages in clandestine intelligence activities in the United States contrary to the interests of the United States, when the circumstances of such person's presence in the United States indicate that such person may engage in such activities in the United States, or when such person knowingly aids or abets any person in the conduct of such activities or knowingly conspires with any person to engage in such activities; or (2) any person who – (A) knowingly engages in clandestine intelligence gathering activities for or on behalf of a foreign power, which activities involve or may involve a violation of the criminal statutes of the United States; (B) pursuant to the direction of an intelligence service or network of a foreign power, knowingly engages in any other clandestine intelligence activities for or on behalf of such foreign power, which activities involve or are about to involve a violation of the criminal statutes of the United States; (C) knowingly engages in sabotage or international terrorism, or activities that are in preparation therefor, or on behalf of a foreign power; (D) knowingly enters the United States under a false or fraudulent identity for or on behalf of a foreign power or, while in the United States, knowingly assumes a false or fraudulent identity for or on behalf of a foreign power; or (E) knowingly aids or abets any person in the conduct of activities described in subparagraph (A), (B), or (C) or knowingly conspires with any person to engage in activities described in subparagraph (A), (B), or (C).

"(c) 'International terrorism' means activities that – (1) involve violent acts or acts dangerous to human life that are a violation of the criminal laws of the United States or of any State, or that would be a criminal violation if committed within the jurisdiction of the United States or any State; (2) appear to be intended – (A) to intimidate or coerce a civilian population; (B) to influence the policy of a government by intimidation or coercion; or (C) to affect the conduct of a government by assassination or kidnaping; and (3) occur totally outside the United States, or transcend national boundaries in terms of the means by which they are accomplished, the persons they appear intended to coerce or intimidate, or the locale in which their perpetrators operate or seek asylum.

"(d) 'Sabotage' means activities that involve a violation of chapter 105 of Title 18, or that would involve such a violation if committed against the United States.

"(e) 'foreign intelligence information' means – (1) information that relates to, and if concerning a United States person is necessary to, the ability of the United States to protect against – (A) actual or potential attack or other grave hostile acts of a foreign power or an agent of a foreign power; (B) sabotage or international terrorism by a foreign power or an agent of a foreign power; or (C) clandestine intelligence activities by an intelligence service or network of a foreign power or by an agent of a foreign power; or (2) information with respect to a foreign power or foreign territory that relates to, and if concerning a United States person is necessary to – (A) the national defense or the security of the United States; or (B) the conduct of the foreign affairs of the United States," 50 U.S.C. 1801.

[34]Strictly speaking for FISA purposes, a United States person "means a citizen of the United States, an alien lawfully admitted for permanent residence (as defined in section 1101(a)(20) of Title 8), an unincorporated association a substantial number of members of which are citizens of the United States or aliens lawfully admitted for permanent residence, or a corporation which is incorporated in the United States, but does not include a corporation or an association which is a foreign power, as defined in subsection (a)(1), (2), or (3) of this section," 50 U.S.C. 1801(i).

to operate under judicial supervision and tend to be confidential as a matter of law, prudence, and practice.

The Act eases some of the restrictions on foreign intelligence gathering within the United States, and affords the U.S. intelligence community greater access to information unearthed during a criminal investigation, but it also establishes and expands safeguards against official abuse. More specifically, it:

- permits "roving" surveillance (court orders omitting the identification of the particular instrument, facilities, or place where the surveillance is to occur when the court finds the target is likely to thwart identification with particularity)
- increases the number of judges on the FISA court from 7 to 11
- allows application for a FISA surveillance or search order when gathering foreign intelligence is *a significant* reason for the application rather than *the* reason
- authorizes pen register and trap & trace device orders for e-mail as well as telephone conversations
- sanctions court ordered access to any tangible item rather than only business records held by lodging, car rental, and locker rental businesses
- carries a sunset provision
- establishes a claim against the U.S. for certain communications privacy violations by government personnel
- expands the prohibition against FISA orders based solely on an American's exercise of his or her First Amendment rights.

FISA

FISA is in essence a series of procedures available to secure court orders in certain foreign intelligence cases.[35] It operates through the judges of a special court which prior to the Act consisted of seven judges, scattered throughout the country, two of whom were from the Washington, D.C. area. The Act, in section 208, authorizes the appointment of four additional judges and requires that three members of the court reside within twenty miles of the District of Columbia, 50 U.S.C. 1803(a).

Search and Surveillance for Intelligence Purposes

Unless directed at a foreign power, the maximum duration for FISA surveillance orders and extensions was once ninety days and forty-five days for physical search orders and extensions, 50 U.S.C. 1805(e), 1824(d)(2000 ed.). The Act, in section 207, extends the maximum tenure of physical search orders to ninety days and in the case of both surveillance orders and physical search orders extends the maximum life of an order involving an agent of a foreign power to 120 days, with extensions for up to a year, 50 U.S.C. 1805(e), 1824(d). This represents a compromise over the Justice Department's original proposal which would have set the required expiration date for orders at one year instead of 120 days, *Draft* at §151.[36]

Section 901 of the Act address a concern raised during the 106th Congress relating to the availability of the FISA orders and the effective use of information gleaned from the execution of a FISA order.[37] It vests the

---

[35]For a general discussion of FISA prior to enactment of the Act, *see*, Bazan, *The Foreign Intelligence Surveillance Act: An Overview of the Statutory Framework for Electronic Surveillance*, CRS REP.NO. RL30465 (Sept. 18, 2001).

[36]*See also, DoJ* at §151, "This section reforms a critical aspect of the Foreign Intelligence Surveillance Act (FISA). It will enable the Foreign Intelligence Surveillance Court (FISC), which presides over applications made by the U.S. government under FISA, to authorize the search and surveillance in the U.S. of officers and employees of foreign powers and foreign members of international terrorist groups for up to a year. Currently, the FISC may only authorize such searches and surveillance for up to 45 days and 90 days, respectively. The proposed change would bring the authorization period in line with that allowed for search and surveillance of the foreign establishments for which the foreign officers and employees work. The proposed change would have no effect on electronic surveillance of U.S. citizens or permanent resident aliens."

Section 314 of the Intelligence Authorization Act for Fiscal Year 2002 (Intelligence Authorization Act), P.L. 107-108, 115 Stat. 1394, 1402 (2001), further amended some of the time limits relating to FISA surveillance and physical searches, extending from 24 hours to 72 hours: (a) the time period during which agents might disseminate or use information secured pursuant to a FISA surveillance or search order but otherwise protected from dissemination or use by the order's minimization requirements; and (b) the permissible duration of emergency surveillance or searches after which surveillance or the search must stop or a FISA order application filed (50 U.S.C. 1801(h)(4), 1821(4)(D), 1805(f), 1824(e)).

[37]*See e.g.*, S.Rep.No. 106-352, at 3, 6, 7 (2000)("The Office of Intelligence Policy and Review (OIPR) in the Department of Justice is responsible for advising the Attorney General on matters relating to the national security of the United States. As part of its responsibilities, the OIPR prepares and presents to the Foreign Intelligence Surveillance Court (FISC) all applications for electronic surveillance and physical searches under the Foreign Intelligence Surveillance Act.... Agencies have informed the Committee that the FISA application process, as interpreted by the OIPR is administratively burdensome and, at times, extremely slow. Many applications undergo months of scrutiny before submission to the court because the OIPR prescribes standards and restrictions not imposed by the statute.... In particular, the OIPR has been criticized for an overly restrictive interpretation of the FISA 'currency' requirement. This is the issue of how recent a subject's activities must be to support a finding of probable cause that the subject is engaged in clandestine intelligence gathering activities.... While existing law does not specifically address "past activities," it does

Director of Central Intelligence with the responsibility to formulate requirements and priorities for the use of FISA to collect foreign intelligence information. He is also charged with the responsibility of assisting the Attorney General in the efficient and effective dissemination of FISA generated information (50 U.S.C. 403-3(c)).

Pen Registers and Trap and Trace Devices for Intelligence Gathering

Section 214 grants the request of the Department of Justice by dropping requirements which limited FISA pen register and trap and trace device orders to facilities used by foreign agents or those engaged in international terrorist or clandestine intelligence activities, 50 U.S.C. 1842(c)(3)(2000 ed.).[38] It is enough that the order is sought as part of an investigation to protect against international terrorism or clandestine intelligence activities and is not motivated solely by an American's exercise of his or her First Amendment rights. Elsewhere (section 505), the Act drops a similar limitation for intelligence officials' access to telephone records, 18 U.S.C. 2709(b), and under the Right to Financial Privacy Act, 12 U.S.C. 3414(a)(5)(A), as well as the Fair Credit Reporting Act, 15 U.S.C. 1681u.[39]

---

notpreclude, and legislative history supports, the conclusion that past activities may be part of the totality of circumstances considered by the FISC in making a probable cause determination.... By definition, information collected pursuant to a court order issued under the Foreign Intelligence Surveillance Act is foreign intelligence not law enforcement information. Accordingly, the Committee wants to clarify that the FISA 'take' can and must be shared by the Federal Bureau of Investigation with appropriate intelligence agencies. For the intelligence mission of the United States to be successful, there must be a cooperative and concerted effort among intelligence agencies. Any information collected by one agency under foreign intelligence authorities that could assist another agency in executing its lawful mission should be shared fully and promptly. Only then can the United States Government pursue aggressively important national security targets including, for example, counterterrorist and counternarcotics targets"); *see also*, 147 *Cong.Rec.* S799-803 (daily ed. Feb. 24, 2000)(remarks of Sens. Specter, Torricelli and Biden).

[38] "When added to FISA two years ago, the pen register/trap and trace section was intended to mirror the criminal pen/trap authority defined in 18 U.S.C. §3123. The FISA authority differs from the criminal authority in that it requires, in addition to a showing of relevance, an additional factual showing that the communications device has been used to contact an 'agent of a foreign power' engaged in international terrorism or clandestine intelligence activities. This has the effect of making the FISA pen/trap authority much more difficult to obtain. In fact, the process of obtaining FISA pen/trap authority is only slightly less burdensome than the process for obtaining full electronic surveillance authority under FISA. This stands in stark contrast to the criminal pen/trap authority, which can be obtained quickly from a local court, on the basis of a certification that the information to be obtained is relevant to an ongoing investigation. The amendment simply eliminates the 'agent of a foreign power' prong from the predication, and thus makes the FISA authority more closely track the criminal authority," *DoJ* at §155.

[39] Except in the case of certain credit information, these are not court procedures, but written requests for third party records which would otherwise to be entitled to confidentiality.

Section 214 adjusts the language of the FISA pen register-trap and trace authority to permit its use to capture source and destination information relating to electronic communications (*e.g.*, e-mail) as well as telephone communications, 50 U.S.C. 1842(d). The section makes it clear that requests for a FISA pen register-trap and trace order, like requests for other FISA orders, directed against Americans (U.S. persons) may not be based solely on activities protected by the First Amendment, 50 U.S.C. 1842, 1843.

Third Party Cooperation and Tangible Evidence

As in the case of criminal investigations, the Act has several sections designed to encourage third party cooperation and to immunize third parties from civil liability for their assistance. FISA orders may include instructions directing specifically identified third parties to assist in the execution of the order, 50 U.S.C. 1805(c)(2)(B). The Act permits inclusion of a general directive for assistance when the target's activities are designed to prevent more specific identification, section 206, and immunizes in 50 U.S.C. 1805(h), those who provide such assistance, section 225.[40]

Section 505, in response to the Justice Department's suggestion, allows FBI field offices to make the requests, *see DoJ* at §157 ("At the present time, National Security Letter (NSL) authority exists in three separate statutes: the Electronic Communications Privacy Act (for telephone and electronic communications records), the Financial Right to Privacy Act (for financial records), and the Fair Credit Reporting Act (for credit records). Like the FISA pen register/trap and trace authority described above, NSL authority requires both a showing of relevance and a showing of links to an 'agent of a foreign power.' In this respect, they are substantially more demanding than the analogous criminal authorities, which require only a certification of relevance. Because the NSLs require documentation of the facts supporting the 'agent of a foreign power' predicate and because they require the signature of a high-ranking official at FBI headquarters, they often take months to be issued. This is in stark contrast to criminal subpoenas, which can be used to obtain the same information, and are issued rapidly at the local level. In many cases, counterintelligence and counterterrorism investigations suffer substantial delays while waiting for NSLs to be prepared, returned from headquarters, and served. The section would streamline the process of obtaining NSL authority, and also clarify the FISA Court can issue orders compelling production of consumer reports").

[40]When it requested the amendment, the Department of Justice explained that the "provision expands the obligations of third parties to furnish assistance to the government under FISA. Under current FISA provisions, the government can seek information and assistance from common carriers, landlords, custodians and other persons specified in court-ordered surveillance. Section 152 would amend FISA to expand existing authority to allow, 'in circumstances where the Court finds that the actions of the target of the application may have the effect of thwarting the identification of a specified person that a common carrier, landlord, custodian or other persons not specified in the Court's order be required to furnish the applicant information and technical assistance necessary to accomplish electronic surveillance in a manner that will protect its secrecy and produce a minimum of interference with the services that such person is providing to the target of electronic surveillance.' This would enhance the FBI's ability to monitor international terrorists and intelligence officers who are trained to thwart surveillance by rapidly changing hotel accommodations, cell

Prior to the Act, FISA allowed federal intelligence officers to seek a court order for access to certain car rental, storage, and hotel accommodation records, 50 U.S.C. 1861 to 1863 (2000 ed.). The Justice Department asked that the authority be replaced with permission to issue administrative subpoenas for any tangible item regardless of the business (if any) of the custodian.[41] The Act amends the provisions, preserving the court order requirement. Yet it allows the procedure to be used in foreign intelligence investigations, conducted to protect against international terrorism or clandestine intelligence activities,[42] in order to seize any tangible item regardless of who is in possession of the item, and continues in place the immunity for good faith compliance by third party custodians, section 215.

In a related provision, Section 358 amends the –

- purposes section of the Currency and Foreign Transaction Reporting Act (31 U.S.C. 5311);
- suspicious activities reporting requirements section of that Act (31 U.S.C. 5318(g)(4)(B);
- availability of records section of that Act (31 U.S.C. 5319);
- purposes section of the Bank Secrecy Act (12 U.S.C. 1829b(a);
- the Secretary of the Treasury's authority over uninsured banks and other financial institutions under that Act (12 U.S.C. 1953(a);
- access provisions of the Right to Financial Privacy Act (12 U.S.C. 3412(2)(a), 3414(a)(1), 3420(a)(2); and

phones, Internet accounts, etc., just prior to important meetings or communications. Under the current law, the government would have to return to the FISA Court for an order that named the new carrier, landlord, etc., before effecting surveillance. Under the proposed amendment, the FBI could simply present the newly discovered carrier, landlord, custodian or other person with a generic order issued by the Court and could then effect FISA coverage as soon as technically feasible," *DoJ* at 152.

Section 314 of the Intelligence Authorization Act immunizes those who assist in the execution of either a FISA surveillance or physical search order (50 U.S.C. 1805(i)), 115 Stat. 1402.

[41] "The 'business records' section of FISA (50 U.S.C. §§1861 and 1862) requires a formal pleading to the Court and the signature of a FISA judge (or magistrate). In practice, this makes the authority unavailable for most investigative contexts. The time and difficulty involved in getting such pleadings before the Court usually outweighs the importance of the business records sought. Since its enactment, the authority has been sought less than five times. This section would delete the old authority and replace it with a general 'administrative subpoena' authority for documents and records. This authority, modeled on the administrative subpoena authority available to drug investigators pursuant to Title 21, allows the Attorney General to compel production of such records upon a finding that the information is relevant," *DoJ* at §156.

[42] Section 314 of the Intelligence Authorization Act further amended the section to permit orders relating to investigations "to obtain foreign intelligence information not concerning a United States person" in addition to those conducted to protect against terrorism and clandestine activities, 50 U.S.C. 1861(a)(1).

- access provisions of the Fair Credit Reporting Act (15 U.S.C. 1681u, 1681v; to clarify and authorize access of federal intelligence authorities to the reports and information gathered and protected under those Acts.[43]

Access to Law Enforcement Information

Shortly after September 11, sources within both Congress and the Administration stressed the need for law enforcement and intelligence agencies to more effectively share information about terrorists and their activities. On September 14, the Senate Select Committee on Intelligence observed that, "effective sharing of information between and among the various components of the government-wide effort to combat terrorists is also essential, and is presently hindered by cultural, bureaucratic, resource, training and, in some cases, legal obstacles," H.R.Rep.No. 107-63, at 10 (2001). The Justice Department's consultation draft of September 20 offered three sections which would have greatly expanded the intelligence

[43]H.R.Rep.No. 107-205, at 60-1 (2001) ("This section clarifies the authority of the Secretary of the Treasury to share Bank Secrecy Act information with the intelligence community for intelligence or counterintelligence activities related to domestic or international terrorism. Under current law, the Secretary may share BSA information with the intelligence community for the purpose of investigating and prosecuting terrorism. This section would make clear that the intelligence community may use this information for purposes unrelated to law enforcement.

"The provision would also expand a Right to Financial Privacy Act (RFPA) exemption, currently applicable to law enforcement inquiries, to allow an agency or department to share relevant financial records with another agency or department involved in intelligence or counterintelligence activities, investigations, or analyses related to domestic or international terrorism. The section would also exempt from most provisions of the RFPA a government authority engaged in investigations of or analyses related to domestic or international terrorism. This section would also authorize the sharing of financial records obtained through a Federal grand jury subpoena when relevant to intelligence or counterintelligence activities, investigations, or analyses related to domestic or international terrorism. In each case, the transferring governmental entity must certify that there is reason to believe that the financial records are relevant to such an activity, investigation, or analysis.

"Finally, this section facilitates government access to information contained in suspected terrorists' credit reports when the governmental inquiry relates to an investigation of, or intelligence activity or analysis relating to, domestic or international terrorism. Even though private entities such as lenders and insurers can access an individual's credit history, the government is strictly limited in its ability under current law to obtain the information. This section would permit those investigating suspected terrorists prompt access to credit histories that may reveal key information about the terrorist's plan or source of funding–without notifying the target. To obtain the information, the governmental authority must certify to the credit bureau that the information is necessary to conduct a terrorism investigation or analysis. The amendment would also create a safe harbor from liability for credit bureaus acting in good faith that comply with a government agency's request for information").

community's access to information collected as part of a criminal investigation. First, it suggested that information generated through the execution of a Title III order might be shared in connection with the duties of any executive branch official, *Draft* at §103.[44]

Second, it recommended a change in Rule 6(e) of the Federal Rules of Criminal Procedure that would allow disclosure of grand jury material to intelligence officials, *Draft* at §354.[45]

Third, it proposed elimination of all constraints on sharing foreign intelligence information uncovered during a law enforcement investigation, mentioning by name the constraints in Rule 6(e) and Title III, *Draft* at §154.[46]

The Act combines versions of all three in section 203. Perhaps because of the nature of the federal grand jury, resolution of the grand jury provision proved especially difficult. The federal grand jury is an exceptional

[44] *See also, DoJ* at §103, "This section facilities the disclosure of Title III information to other components of the intelligence community in terrorism investigations. At present, 18 U.S.C. §2517(1) generally allows information obtained via wiretap to be disclosed only to the extent that it will assist a criminal investigation. One must obtain a court order to disclose Title III information in non-criminal proceedings. Section 109 [103] would modify the wiretap statutes to permit the disclosure of Title III generated information to a non-law enforcement officer for such purposes as furthering an intelligence investigation. This will harmonize Title III standards with those of the Foreign Intelligence Surveillance Act (FISA), which allows such information-sharing. Allowing disclosure under Title III is particularly appropriate given that the requirements for obtaining a Title III surveillance order in general are more stringent than for a FISA order, and because the attendant privacy concerns in either situation are similar and are adequately protected by existing statutory provisions."

[45] *See also, DoJ* at §354, "This section makes changes in Rule 6(e) of the Federal Rules of Criminal Procedure, relating to grand jury secrecy, to facilitate the sharing of information with federal law enforcement, intelligence, protective, national defense, and immigration personnel in terrorism and national security cases. The section is in part complimentary to section 154 of the bill, relating to sharing of foreign intelligence information, and reflects a similar purpose of promoting a coordinated governmental response to terrorist and national security threats." Contrary to the implication here section 154 deals with sharing information gathered by law enforcement officials not with information gathered by intelligence officers

[46] *See also, DoJ* at §154, "This section provides that foreign intelligence information obtained in criminal investigations, including grand jury and electronic surveillance information, may be shared with other federal government personnel having responsibilities relating to the defense of the nation and its interests. With limited exceptions, it is presently impossible for criminal investigators to share information obtained through a grand jury (including through the use of grand jury subpoenas) and information obtained from electronic surveillance authorized under Title III with the intelligence community. This limitation will be very significant in some criminal investigations. For example, grand jury subpoenas often are used to obtain telephone, computer, financial and other business records in organized crime investigations. Thus, these relatively basic investigative materials are inaccessible for examination by intelligence community analysts working on related transnational organized crime groups. A similar problem occurs in computer intrusion investigations: grand jury subpoenas and Title III intercepts are used to collect transactional data and to monitor the

institution. Its purpose is to determine if a crime has been committed, and if so by whom; to indict the guilty; and to refuse to indict the innocent. Its probes may begin without probable cause or any other threshold of suspicion.[47] It examines witnesses and evidence ordinarily secured in its name and questioned before it by Justice Department prosecutors. Its affairs are conducted in private and outside the presence of the court. Only the attorney for the government, witnesses under examination, and a court reporter may attend its proceedings, F.R.Crim.P. 6(d). Matters occurring before the grand jury are secret and may be disclosed by the attending attorney for the government and those assisting the grand jury only in the performance of their duties; in presentation to a successor grand jury; or under court order for judicial proceedings, for inquiry into misconduct before the grand jury, or for state criminal proceedings, F.R.Crim.P. 6(e).

The Act, in section 203(a), allows disclosure of matters occurring before the grand jury to "any federal law enforcement, intelligence, protective, immigration, national defense, or national security" officer to assist in the performance of his official duties, F.R.Crim.P. 6(e)(3)(C)(i)(V).[48]

Critics may protest that the change could lead to the use of the grand jury for intelligence gathering purposes, or less euphemistically, to spy on Americans.[49] The proposal was never among those scheduled to sunset, but

---

unknown intruders. The intelligence community will have an equal interest in such information, because the intruder may be acting on behalf of a foreign power."

[47] *Blair v. United States*, 250 U.S. 273, 281 (1919)(the grand jury "is a grand inquest, a body with powers of investigation and inquisition, the scope of whose inquiries is not to be limited narrowly by questions of propriety or forecasts of whether any particular individual will be found properly subject to an accusation of crime").

[48] These officers may receive: (1) "foreign intelligence information" that is, information regardless whether it involves Americans or foreign nationals that "[a] relates to the ability of the United States to protect against – (aa) actual or potential attack or other grave hostile acts of a foreign power or an agent of a foreign power; (bb) sabotage or international terrorism by a foreign power or an agent of a foreign power; (cc) clandestine intelligence activities by an intelligence service or network of a foreign power," or [b] "with respect to a foreign power or foreign territory that relates to – (aa) the national defense or security of the United States; or (bb) the conduct of the foreign affairs of the United States," F.R.Crim.P. 6(e)(3)(C)(iv); (2) when the matters involve foreign intelligence or counterintelligence, that is, [a] "information relating to the capabilities, intentions, or activities of foreign governments or elements thereof, foreign organizations, or foreign persons, or international terrorist activities" or [b] "information gathered and activities conducted, to protect against espionage, other intelligence activities, sabotage, or assassinations conducted on behalf of foreign governments or elements thereof, foreign organizations, or foreign persons, *or international terrorist activities*," 50 U.S.C. 401a(2),(3)(language added by section 902 of the Act in italics).

[49] Beale & Felman, The Consequences of Enlisting Federal Grand Juries in the War on Terrorism: Assessing the USA PATRIOT Act's Changes to Grand Jury Secrecy, 25 HARVARD JOURNAL OF LAW & PUBLIC POLICY 699, 719-20 (2002)("There is a significant danger that the rule permitting disclosure will be treated as the de facto

earlier versions of the section followed the path used for most other disclosures of grand jury material: prior court approval, H.R.Rep.No. 107-236, at 73 (2001). The Act, in section 203(a), instead calls for confidential notification of the court that a disclosure has occurred and the entity to whom it was made, F.R.Crim.P. 6(e)(3)(C)(iii). It also insists that the Attorney General establish implementing procedures for instances when the disclosure "identifies" Americans (U.S. persons), section 203(c).

Law enforcement officials may share Title III information with the intelligence community under the same conditions, section 203(b),[50] although the grand jury and Title III sharing provisions differ in at least three important respects. The court need not be notified of Title III disclosures. On the other hand, the authority for sharing Title III information expires on December 31, 2005, section 224, and agencies and their personnel guilty of intentional improper disclosures may be subject to a claim for damages and disciplinary action, 18 U.S.C. 2520.

---

authorization of an expansion of the grand jury's investigative role to encompass seeking material relevant only to matters of national security, national defense, immigration, and so forth. The grand jury's awesome powers should not be unwittingly extended to a much wider range of issues... Since the grand jury operates in secret, there are no public checks on the scope of its investigations, and witnesses are not permitted to challenge its jurisdiction. Only the supervising court is in a position to keep the grand jury's investigation within proper bounds. Requiring judicial approval of foreign intelligence and counterintelligence information disclosures would provide a natural check against the temptation to manipulate the grand jury to develop information for unauthorized purposes"); but see, Scheidegger et al., Federalist Society White Paper on The USA PATRIOT Act of 2001: Criminal Procedure Sections 6 (Nov.2001)("The grand jury secrecy rule is a rule of policy which has always had exceptions, and it has been frequently modified. The secrecy rule has no credible claim to constitutional stature").

[50]Information derived from a Title III interception may be shared with any other federal law enforcement, intelligence, protective, immigration, national defense, or national security officer if it regards: (1) "foreign intelligence information" that is, information irrespective of whether it involves Americans or foreign nationals that "[A] relates to the ability of the United States to protect against – (i) actual or potential attack or other grave hostile acts of a foreign power or an agent of a foreign power; (ii) sabotage or international terrorism by a foreign power or an agent of a foreign power; (iii) clandestine intelligence activities by an intelligence service or network of a foreign power;" or [B] "with respect to a foreign power or foreign territory that relates to – (i) the national defense or security of the United States; or (ii) the conduct of the foreign affairs of the United States;" (2) when the matters involve foreign intelligence or counterintelligence as defined by 50 U.S.C. 401a (as amended by section 902 of the Act), *i.e.*, "As used in this Act: (1) The term 'intelligence' includes foreign intelligence and counterintelligence. (2) The term 'foreign intelligence' means information relating to the capabilities, intentions, or activities of foreign governments or elements thereof, foreign organizations, or foreign persons, *or international terrorist activities*. (3) The term 'counterintelligence' means information gathered and activities conducted, to protect against espionage, other intelligence activities, sabotage, or assassinations conducted by or on behalf of foreign governments or elements thereof, foreign organizations, or foreign persons, or international terrorist activities" (language added by section 902 in italics).

The third subsection of section 203 remains something of an enigma. It speaks in much the same language as its counterparts. It allows law enforcement officials to share information with the intelligence community, "notwithstanding any other provisions of law," section 203(d).[51] It either swallows the other subsections, or supplements them. Several factors argue for its classification as a supplement. Congress is unlikely to have crafted subsections (a), (b) and (c) only to completely nullify them in subsection (d). Without a clear indication to the contrary, the courts are unlikely to find that Congress intended nullification.[52] By gathering the three into a single section Congress avoided the suggestion that the phrase "notwithstanding any other provision of law" constitutes surplusage. The Title III and grand jury sharing procedures are not in other provisions of law, they are now subsections of the same provision of law. Moreover, Congress seemed to signal an intent for the subsections to operate in tandem when it dropped the language of the original Justice Department proposal which expressly identified Title III and Rule 6(e) as examples of the restrictions to be overcome by the universal sharing language.[53]

---

[51]"Notwithstanding any other provision of law, it shall be lawful for foreign intelligence or counterintelligence (as defined in section 3 of the National Security Act of 1947 (50 U.S.C.) or foreign intelligence information obtained as part of a criminal investigation to be disclosed to any federal law enforcement, intelligence, protective, immigration, national defense, or national security official in order to assist the official receiving that information in the performance of his official duties. Any federal official who receives information pursuant to this provision may use that information only as necessary in the conduct of that person's official duties subject to any limitations on the unauthorized disclosure of such information," §203(d)(1). The subsection goes to define "foreign intelligence information" in the same terms used to define that phrase in Title III (18 U.S.C. 2510(19)) and in Rule 6(e)(F.R.Crim.P.6(e)(3)(C)(iv)), §203(d)(2).

[52]*Duncan v. Walker*, 121 S.Ct. 2120, 2125 (2001)(internal quotation marks and parallel citations omitted)("It is our duty to give effect, if possible, to every clause and word of a statute. *United States v. Menasche*, 348 U.S. 528, 538-539 (1955) (quoting *Montclair v. Ramsdell*, 107 U.S. 147, 152(1883)); see also *Williams v. Taylor*, 529 U.S. 362, 404 (2000) (describing this rule as a cardinal principle of statutory construction); *Market Co. v. Hoffman*, 101 U.S. 112, 115 (1879)(As early as in Bacon's Abridgment, sect. 2, it was said that a statute ought, upon the whole, to be so construed that, if it can be prevented, no clause, sentence, or word shall be superfluous, void, or insignificant). We are thus reluctant to treat statutory terms as surplusage in any setting. *Babbitt v. Sweet Home Chapter, Communities for Great Ore.*, 515 U.S. 687, 698 (1995); see also *Ratzlaf v. United States*, 510 U.S. 135, 140 (1994)").

It is not possible to conclude that Congress intended the universal subsection (d) to apply until sunset and the grand jury and Title III subsections (a), (b), and (c) to operate thereafter, because the Title III subsection expires at the same time as the universal subsection.

[53]*Draft* at §154, "Notwithstanding any other provision of law, it shall be lawful for foreign intelligence information obtained as part of a criminal investigation (including, without limitation, information subject to Rule 6(e) of the Federal Rules of Criminal Procedure and information obtained pursuant to chapter 119 of title 18, United States Code [*i.e.* Title III]) to be provided to any federal law enforcement, intelligence, protective, or national defense

Section 203 deals with earlier legal impediments to sharing foreign intelligence information unearthed during the course of a criminal investigation. Section 905 looks to dissolve the barriers may be more cultural than legal. Under it, the Attorney General is to issue guidelines governing the transmittal to the Director of Central Intelligence of foreign intelligence information that surfaces in the course of a criminal investigation. The section also instructs the Attorney General to promulgate guidelines covering reports to the Director of Central Intelligence on whether a criminal investigation has been initiated or declined based on an intelligence community referral, 50 U.S.C. 403-5b. To ensure effective use of increased information sharing, section 908 calls for training of federal, state and local officials to enable them to recognize foreign intelligence information which they encounter in their work and how to use it in the performance of their duties, 28 U.S.C. 509 note.

Increasing Institutional Capacity

As noted elsewhere, the Act liberalizes authority for the FBI to hire translators, section 203, which enhances its capacity to conduct both criminal and foreign intelligence investigations. The Act also reflects sentiments expressed earlier concerning coordinated efforts to develop a computerized translation capability to be used in foreign intelligence gathering.[54] Section

personnel, or any federal personnel responsible for administering the immigration laws of the United States, or to the President and the Vice President of the United States."

[54] "The Committee is concerned that intelligence in general, and intelligence related to terrorism in particular, is increasingly reliant on the ability of the Intelligence Community to quickly, accurately and efficiently translate information in a large number of languages. Many of the languages for which translation capabilities are limited within the United States Government are the languages that are of critical importance in our counterterrorism efforts. The Committee believes that this problem can be alleviated by applying cutting-edge, internet-like technology to create a 'National Virtual Translation Center.' Such a center would link secure locations maintained by the Intelligence Community throughout the country and would apply digital technology to network, store, retrieve, and catalogue the audio and textual information. Foreign intelligence could be collected technically in one location, translated in a second location, and provided to an Intelligence Community analyst in a third location.

"The Committee notes that the CIA, FBI NSA and other intelligence agencies have applied new technology to this problem. The Committee believes that these efforts should be coordinated so that the solution can be applied on a Community-wide basis. Accordingly, the Committee directs the Director of Central Intelligence, in consultation with the Director of the FBI, and other heads of departments and agencies within the Intelligence Community, to prepare and submit to the intelligence committees by June 1, 2002, a report concerning the feasibility and structure of a National Virtual Translation Center, including recommendations regarding the

907 instructs the Director of the Central Intelligence, in consultation with the Director of the FBI, to report on the creation of a National Virtual Translation Center. The report is to include information concerning staffing, allocation of resources, compatibility with comparable systems to be used for law enforcement purposes, and features which permit its efficient and secure use by all of the intelligence agencies.

MONEY LAUNDERING

In federal law, money laundering is the flow of cash or other valuables derived from, or intended to facilitate, the commission of a criminal offense. It is the movement of the fruits and instruments of crime. Federal authorities attack money laundering through regulations, international cooperation, criminal sanctions, and forfeiture.[55] The Act bolsters federal efforts in each area.

Regulation

Prior to passage of the Act, the Treasury Department already enjoyed considerable authority to impose reporting and record-keeping standards on financial institutions generally and with respect to anti-money laundering matters in particular.[56]

Records and Reports

For instance, under the Currency and Financial Transaction Reporting Act, a component of the Bank Secrecy Act, anyone who transports more than $10,000 into or out of the United States must report that fact to the Treasury Department, 31 U.S.C. 5316. Banks, credit unions, and certain other financial institutions must likewise report identifying information relating to cash transactions in excess of $10,000 to the Treasury Department (CTRs), 31 U.S.C. 5313, 31 C.F.R. §103.22. Other businesses are required to report

establishment of such a center and the funding necessary to do so," S.Rep.No. 107-63, at 11 (2001).

[55]For a brief overview, *see*, Murphy, *Money Laundering: Current Law and Proposals*, CRS REP.NO. RS21032 (DEC. 21, 2001).

[56]*See e.g.*, 12 U.S.C. 1829b (retention or records by insured depository institutions), 1951-1959 (record-keeping by financial institutions); 31 U.S.C. 5311 ("It is the purpose of this subchapter [31 U.S.C. 5311 et seq.] (except section 5315 [relating to foreign current transaction reports]) to require certain reports or records where they have a high degree of usefulness in criminal, tax, or regulatory investigations or proceedings").

to the Internal Revenue Service the particulars relating to any transaction involving more than $10,000 in cash, 26 U.S.C. 60501. Banks must file suspicious activity reports (SARs) with the Treasury Department's Financial Crimes Enforcement Network (FinCEN) for any transactions involving more than $5,000 which they suspect may be derived from illegal activity, 31 U.S.C. 5318(g), 31 C.F.R. §103.18. Money transmission businesses and those that deal in traveler's checks or money orders are under a similar obligation for suspicious activities involving more than $2,000, 31 U.S.C. 5318(g), 31 C.F.R. §103.18.

Among other things, the Act expands the authority of the Secretary of the Treasury over these reporting requirements. He is to promulgate regulations, pursuant to sections 356 and 321, under which securities brokers and dealers as well as commodity merchants, advisors and pool operators must file suspicious activity reports, 31 U.S.C. 5318 note; 31 U.S.C. 5312(2)(c)(1). Businesses which were only to report cash transactions involving more than $10,000 to the IRS are now required to files SARs as well,[57] reflecting Congress' view that the information provided the IRS may be valuable for other law enforcement purposes.[58] This concern is likewise

[57]Section 365, 31 U.S.C. 5331; Sec. 321, 31 U.S.C. 5312.

[58]H.R.Rep.No. 107-250, at 38-9 (2001)("Most importantly, the Committee found significant shortcomings in the use of information already in possession of the government. Section 60501 of the Internal Revenue Code requires that any person engaged in a trade or business (other than financial institutions required to report under the Bank Secrecy Act) file a report with the Federal government on cash transactions in excess of $10,000. Reports filed pursuant to this requirement provide law enforcement authorities with a paper trail that can, among other things, lead to the detection and prosecution of money laundering activity.

"Under current law, non-financial institutions are required to report cash transactions exceeding $10,000 to the Internal Revenue Service (IRS) on IRS Form 8300. Because the requirement that such reports be filed is contained in the Internal Revenue Code, Form 8300 information is considered tax return information, and is subject to the procedural and record-keeping requirements of section 6103 of the Internal Revenue Code. For example, section 6103(p)(4)(E) requires agencies seeking Form 8300 information to file a report with the Secretary of the Treasury that describes the procedures established and utilized by the agency for ensuring the confidentiality of the information. IRS requires that agencies requesting Form 8300 information file a 'Safeguard Procedures Report' which must be approved by the IRS before any such information can be released. For that reason, Federal, State and local law enforcement agencies are not given access to the Form 8300s as Congress anticipated when it last amended this statute. See 26 U.S.C. 6103(1)(15).

"While the IRS uses Form 8300 to identify individuals who may be engaged in tax evasion, Form 8300 information can also be instrumental in helping law enforcement authorities trace cash payments by drug traffickers and other criminals for luxury cars, jewelry, and other expensive merchandise. Because of the restrictions on their dissemination outlined above, however, Form 8300s are not nearly as accessible to law enforcement authorities as the various reports mandated by the Bank Secrecy Act, which can typically be retrieved electronically from a database maintained by the Treasury Department. The differential access to the two kinds of reports is made anomalous by the fact that Form 8300 elicits much the same information that is required to be disclosed by the Bank Secrecy Act. For example,

reflected in section 357 which asks the Secretary of the Treasury to report on the Internal Revenue Service's role in the administration of the Currency and Foreign Transaction Reporting Act (31 U.S.C. 5311 et seq.), and what transfers of authority, if any, are appropriate.

Sections 351 and 355 address the liability for disclosure of suspicious activity reports (SARs). Prior to the Act, federal law prohibited financial institutions and their officers and employees from tipping off any of the participants in a suspicious transaction, 31 U.S.C. 5318(g)(2)(2000 ed.). Federal law, however, immunized the institutions and their officers and employees from liability for filing the reports and for failing to disclose that they had done so, 31 U.S.C. 5318(g)(3)(2000 ed.). Section 351 makes changes in both the immunity and the proscription. It adds government officials who have access to the reports to the anti-tip ban, 31 U.S.C. 5318(g)(2)(A). It allows, but does not require, institutions to reveal SAR information in the context of employment references to other financial institutions, 31 U.S.C. 5318(g)(2)(B). Finally, it makes clear that the immunity does not extend to immunity from governmental action.[59] Section

just as Form 8300 seeks the name, address, and social security number of a customer who engages in a cash transaction exceeding $10,000 with a trade or business, Currency Transaction Reports (CTRs) mandated by the Bank Secrecy Act require the same information to be reported on a cash transaction exceeding $10,000 between a financial institution and its customer").

[59]"Subsection (a) of section [351] makes certain technical and clarifying amendments to 31 U.S.C. 5318(g)(3), the Bank Secrecy Act's 'safe harbor' provision that protects financial institutions that disclose possible violations of law or regulation from civil liability for reporting their suspicions and for not alerting those identified in the reports. The safe harbor is directed at Suspicious Activity Reports and similar reports to the government and regulatory authorities under the Bank Secrecy Act.

"First, section [351](a) amends section 5318(g)(3) to make clear that the safe harbor from civil liability applies in arbitration, as well as judicial, proceedings, Second, it amends section 5318(g)(3) to clarify the safe harbor's coverage of voluntary disclosures (that is, those not covered by the SAR regulatory reporting requirement). The language in section 5318(g)(3)(A) providing that 'any financial institution that * * * makes a disclosure pursuant to * * * any other authority * * * shall not be liable to any person' is not intended to avoid the application of the reporting and disclosure provisions of the Federal securities laws to any person, or to insulate any issuers from private rights of actions for disclosures made under the Federal securities laws.

"Subsection [351](b) amends section 5318(g)(2) of title 31--which currently prohibits notification of any person involved in a transaction reported in a SAR that a SAR has been filed--to clarify (1) that any government officer or employee who learns that a SAR has been filed may not disclose that fact to any person identified in the SAR, except as necessary to fulfill the officer or employee's official duties, and (2) that disclosure by a financial institution of potential wrongdoing in a written employment reference provided in response to a request from another financial institution pursuant to section 18(v) of the Federal Deposit Insurance Act, or in a written termination notice or employment reference provided in accordance with the rules of a securities self-regulatory organization, is not prohibited

355 expands the immunity to cover disclosures in employment references to other insured depository financial institutions provided disclosure is not done with malicious intent.[60]

The Financial Crimes Enforcement Network (FinCEN), a component within the Treasury Department long responsible for these anti-money laundering reporting and record-keeping requirements, 31 C.F.R. pt. 103, was administratively created in 1990 to provide other government agencies with an "intelligence and analytical network in support of the detection, investigation, and prosecution of domestic and international money laundering and other financial crimes," 55 *Fed.Reg.* 18433 (May 2, 1990).

The Act, in section 361, makes FinCEN a creature of statute, a bureau within the Treasury Department, 31 U.S.C. 310. Section 362 charges it with the responsibility of establishing a highly secure network to allow financial institutions to file required reports electronically and to permit FinCEN to provide those institutions with alerts and other information concerning money laundering protective measures, 31 U.S.C. 310 note.

Special Measure

In extraordinary circumstances involving international financial matters, the Act grants the Secretary of the Treasury, in consultation with other appropriate regulatory authorities, the power to issue regulations and orders involving additional required "special measures" and additional "due diligence" requirements to combat money laundering. The special measure authority, available under section 311, comes to life with the determination that particular institutions, jurisdictions, types of accounts, or types of transactions pose a primary money laundering concern.[61] These special measures may require U.S. financial institutions to:

---

simply because the potential wrongdoing was also reported in a SAR," H.R.Rep.No. 107-250, at 66 (2001).

[60] 31 U.S.C. 1828(w). "This section deals with the same employment reference issue addressed in section [351] but with respect to title 12. Occasionally banks develop suspicions that a bank officer or employee has engaged in potentially unlawful activity. These suspicions typically result in the bank filing a SAR. Under present law, however, the ability of banks to share these suspicions in written employment references with other banks when such an officer or employee seeks new employment is unclear. Section 208 would amend 12 U.S.C. 1828 to permit a bank, upon request by another bank, to share information in a written employment reference concerning the possible involvement of a current or former officer or employee in potentially unlawful activity without fear of civil liability for sharing the information, but only to the extent that the disclosure does not contain information which the bank knows to be false, and the bank has not acted with malice or with reckless disregard for the truth in making the disclosure," H.R.Rep.No. 107-250, at 67 (2001).

[61] 31 U.S.C. 5318A. The circumstances considered in the case of a suspect jurisdiction are: evidence of organized crime or terrorist transactions there; the extent to which the jurisdiction's bank secrecy or other regulatory practices encourage foreign use; the extent

- maintain more extensive records and submit additional reports relating to participants in foreign financial transactions with which they are involved
- secure beneficial ownership information with respect to accounts maintained for foreign customers
- adhere to "know-your-customer" requirements concerning foreign customers who use "payable-through accounts" held by the U.S. entity for foreign financial institutions
- keep identification records on foreign financial institutions' customers whose transactions are routed through the foreign financial institution's correspondent accounts with the U.S. financial institution
- honor limitations on correspondent or payable-through accounts maintained for foreign financial institutions.[62]

---

and effectiveness of the jurisdiction's banking regulation; the volume of financial transactions in relation to the size of the jurisdiction's economy; whether international watch dog groups (such as the Financial Action Task Force) have identified the jurisdiction as an offshore banking or secrecy haven; the existence or absence of a mutual legal assistance treaty between the U.S. and the jurisdiction; and the extent of official corruption within the jurisdiction. The institutional circumstances weighed before imposing special measures with respect to particular institutions or types of accounts or transactions include the intent to which the suspect institution or types of accounts or transactions are particularly attractive to money launderers, the extent to which they can be used by legitimate businesses, and the extent to which focused measures are likely to be successful.

[62]The House report describes these measures in greater detail: "Section [311] adds a new section 5318A to the Bank Secrecy Act, authorizing the Secretary of the Treasury to require domestic financial institutions and agencies to take one or more of five 'special measures' if the Secretary finds that reasonable grounds exist to conclude that a foreign jurisdiction, a financial institution operating outside the United States, a class of international transactions, or one or more types of accounts is a 'primary money laundering concern.' Prior to invoking any of the special measures contained in section 5318A(b), the Secretary is required to consult with the Chairman of the Board of Governors of the Federal Reserve System, any other appropriate Federal banking agency, the Securities and Exchange Commission, the National Credit Union Administration Board, and, in the sole discretion of the Secretary, such other agencies and interested parties as the Secretary may find to be appropriate. Among other things, this consultation is designed to ensure that the Secretary possesses information on the effect that any particular special measure may have on the domestic and international banking system. In addition, the Committee encourages the Secretary to consult with non-governmental 'interested parties,' including, for example, the Bank Secrecy Act Advisory Group, to obtain input from those who may be subject to a regulation or order under this section.

"Prior to invoking any of the special measures contained in section 5318A, the Secretary must consider three discrete factors, namely (1) whether other countries or multilateral groups have taken similar action; (2) whether the imposition of the measure would create a significant competitive disadvantage, including any significant cost or burden associated with compliance, for firms organized or licensed in the United States; and (3) the extent to which the action would have an adverse systemic impact on the payment system or legitimate business transactions.

"Finally, subsection (a) makes clear that this new authority is not to be construed as superseding or restricting any other authority of the Secretary or any other agency.

"Subsection (b) of the new section 5318A outlines the five 'special measures' the Secretary may invoke against a foreign jurisdiction, financial institution operating outside the U.S., class of transaction within, or involving, a jurisdiction outside the U.S., or one or more types of accounts, that he finds to be of primary money laundering concern.

"The first such measure would require domestic financial institutions to maintain records and/or file reports on certain transactions involving the primary money laundering concern, to include any information the Secretary requires, such as the identity and address of participants in a transaction, the legal capacity in which the participant is acting, the beneficial ownership of the funds (in accordance with steps that the Secretary determines to be reasonable and practicable to obtain such information), and a description of the transaction. The records and/or reports authorized by this section must involve transactions from a foreign jurisdiction, a financial institution operating outside the United States, or class of international transactions within, or involving, a foreign jurisdiction, and are not to include transactions that both originate and terminate in, and only involve, domestic financial institutions.

"The second special measure would require domestic financial institutions to take such steps as the Secretary determines to be reasonable and practicable to ascertain beneficial ownership of accounts opened or maintained in the U.S. by a foreign person (excluding publicly traded foreign corporations) associated with what has been determined to be a primary money laundering concern.

"The third special measure the Secretary could impose in the case of a primary money laundering concern would require domestic financial institutions, as a condition of opening or maintaining a 'payable-through account' for a foreign financial institution, to identify each customer (and representative of the customer) who is permitted to use or whose transactions flow through such an account, and to obtain for each customer (and representative) information that is substantially comparable to the information it would obtain with respect to its own customers. A 'payable-through account' is defined for purposes of the legislation as an account, including a transaction account (as defined in section 19(b)(1)(C) of the Federal Reserve Act), opened at a depository institution by a foreign financial institution by means of which the foreign financial institution permits its customers to engage, either directly or through a sub-account, in banking activities usual in connection with the business of banking in the United States.

"The fourth special measure the Secretary could impose in the case of a primary money laundering concern would require domestic financial institutions, as a condition of opening or maintaining a 'correspondent' account for a foreign financial institution, to identify each customer (and representative of the customer) who is permitted to use or whose transactions flow through such an account, and to obtain for each customer (and representative) information that is substantially comparable to the information that it would obtain with respect to its own customers. With respect to a bank, the term 'correspondent account' means an account established to receive deposits from and make payments on behalf of a foreign financial institution.

"The fifth measure the Secretary could impose in the case of a primary money laundering concern would prohibit or impose conditions (beyond those already provided for in the third and fourth measures) on domestic financial institutions' correspondent or payable-through accounts with foreign banking institutions. In addition to the required consultation with the Chairman of the Board of Governors of the Federal Reserve, prior to imposing this measure the Secretary is also directed to consult with the Secretary of State and the Attorney General.

"The five special measures authorized by this section may be imposed in any sequence or combination as the Secretary determines. The first four special measures may be imposed by regulation, order, or otherwise as permitted by law. However, if the Secretary proceeds by issuing an order, the order must be accompanied by a notice of proposed rulemaking relating to the imposition of the special measure, and may not remain in effect for more than 120

Due Diligence

Section 312 demands that all U.S. financial institutions have policies, procedures, and controls in place to identify instances where their correspondent and private banking accounts with foreign individuals and entities might be used for money laundering purposes, 31 U.S.C. 5318(i). They must establish enhanced due diligence standards for correspondent accounts held for offshore banking institutions (whose licenses prohibit them from conducting financial activities in the jurisdiction in which they are licensed) or institutions in money laundering jurisdictions designated by the Secretary of the Treasury or by international watch dog groups such as the Financial Action Task Force. The standards must at least involve reasonable efforts to identify the ownership of foreign institutions which are not publicly held; closely monitor the accounts for money laundering activity; and to hold any foreign bank, for whom the U.S. institution has a correspondent account, to the same standards with respect to other correspondent accounts maintained by the foreign bank. In the case of private banking accounts of $1 million or more, U.S. financial institutions must keep records of the owners of the accounts and the source of funds deposited in the accounts. They must report suspicious transactions and, when the accounts are held for foreign officials, guard against transactions involving foreign official corruption.[63]

---

days, except pursuant to a regulation prescribed on or before the end of the 120-day period. The fifth special measure may be imposed only by regulation," H.R.Rep.No. 107-250, at 68-9.

[63] *See generally*, H.R.Rep.No. 107-250, at 71-2 ("Section [312] amends 31 U.S.C. 5318 to require financial institutions that establish, maintain, administer, or manage private banking or correspondent accounts for non-U.S. persons to establish appropriate, specific, and, where necessary, enhanced due diligence policies, procedures, and controls to detect and report instances of money laundering through those accounts.

"The section requires financial institutions to apply enhanced due diligence procedures when opening or maintaining a correspondent account for a foreign bank operating (1) under a license to conduct banking activities which, as a condition of the license, prohibits the licensed entity from conducting banking activities with the citizens of, or with the local currency of, the country which issued the license; or (2) under a license issued by a foreign country that has been designated (a) as non-cooperative with international anti-money laundering principles by an intergovernmental group or organization of which the United States is a member, with which designation the Secretary of the Treasury concurs, or (b) by the Secretary as warranting special measures due to money laundering concerns.

"The enhanced due diligence procedures include (1) ascertaining the identity of each of the owners of the foreign bank (except for banks that are publicly traded); (2) conducting enhanced scrutiny of the correspondent account to guard against money laundering and report any suspicious activity; and (3) ascertaining whether the foreign bank provides correspondent accounts to other foreign banks and, if so, the identity of those foreign banks and related due diligence information.

"For private banking accounts requested or maintained by a non-United States person, a financial institution is required to implement procedures for (1) ascertaining the identity of

General Regulatory Matters

The Act establishes several other regulatory mechanisms directed at the activities involving U.S. financial institutions and foreign individuals or institutions. Section 313, for instance, in another restriction on correspondent accounts for foreign financial institutions, prohibits U.S. financial institutions from maintaining correspondent accounts either directly or indirectly for foreign shell banks (banks with no physical place of business[64]) which have no affiliation with any financial institution through which their banking activities are subject to regulatory supervision.[65]

The Act, in section 325, empowers the Secretary of the Treasury to promulgate regulations to prevent financial institutions from allowing their customers to conceal their financial activities by taking advantage of the institutions' concentration account practices.[66]

---

the nominal and beneficial owners of, and the source of funds deposited into, the account as needed to guard against money laundering and report suspicious activity; and (2) conducting enhanced scrutiny of any such account requested or maintained by, or on behalf of, a senior foreign political figure, or his immediate family members or close associates, to prevent, detect and report transactions that may involve the proceeds of foreign corruption. A private bank account is defined as an account (or any combination of accounts) that requires a minimum aggregate deposit of funds or other assets of not less than $1 million; is established on behalf of one or more individuals who have a direct or beneficial ownership in the account; and is assigned to, or administered or managed by, an officer, employee or agent of a financial institution acting as a liaison between the institution and the direct or beneficial owner of the account.

"This section directs the Secretary of the Treasury, within 6 months of enactment of this bill and in consultation with appropriate Federal functional regulators to further define and clarify, by regulation, the requirements imposed by this section").

[64]Or more exactly, a bank which has no physical presence in any country; a "physical presence" for a foreign bank is defined as "a place of business that – (i) is maintained by a foreign bank; (ii) is located at a fixed address (other than solely an electronic address) in a country in which the foreign bank is authorized to conduct banking activities, at which location the foreign bank – (I) employs 1 or more individuals on a full-time basis; and (II) maintains operating records relating to its banking activities; and (iii) is subject to inspection by the banking authority which licensed the foreign bank to conduct banking activities," 31 U.S.C. 5318(j)(4).

[65]31 U.S.C. 5318(j); H.R.Rep.No. 107-250, at 72 (2001).

[66]The Act does not define "concentration accounts," although the House Financial Services Committee report provides some incite into the section's intent, H.R.Rep.No. 107-250, at 72-3 (2001)("This section gives the Secretary of the Treasury discretionary authority to prescribe regulations governing the maintenance of concentration accounts by financial institutions, to ensure that these accounts are not used to prevent association of the identity of an individual customer with the movement of funds of which the customer is the direct or beneficial owner. If promulgated, the regulations are required to prohibit financial institutions from allowing clients to direct transactions into, out of, or through the concentration accounts of the institution; prohibit financial institutions and their employees from informing customers of the existence of, or means of identifying, the concentration accounts of the institution; and to establish written procedures governing the documentation of all transactions involving a concentration account.")

The Secretary of the Treasury is instructed in section 326 to issue regulations for financial institutions' minimum new customer identification standards and record-keeping and to recommend a means to effectively verify the identification of foreign customers.[67]

---

[67] 31 U.S.C. 5318(*l*); H.R.Rep.No. 107-250, at 62-3 (2001)("Section [326](a) amends 31 U.S.C. 5318 by adding a new subsection governing the identification of account holders. Paragraph (1) directs Treasury to prescribe regulations setting forth minimum standards for customer identification by financial institutions in connection with the opening of an account. By referencing 'customers' in this section, the Committee intends that the regulations prescribed by Treasury take an approach similar to that of regulations promulgated under title V of the Gramm-Leach-Bliley Act of 1999, where the functional regulators defined 'customers' and 'customer relationship' for purposes of the financial privacy rules. Under this approach, for example, where a mutual fund sells its shares to the public through a broker-dealer and maintains a 'street name' or omnibus account in the broker-dealer's name, the individual purchasers of the fund shares are customers of the broker-dealer, rather than the mutual fund. The mutual fund would not be required to 'look through' the broker-dealer to identify and verify the identities of those customers. Similarly, where a mutual fund sells its shares to a qualified retirement plan, the plan, and not its participants, would be the fund's customers. Thus, the fund would not be required to 'look through' the plan to identify its participants.

"Paragraph (2) requires that the regulations must, at a minimum, require financial institutions to implement procedures to verify (to the extent reasonable and practicable) the identity of any person seeking to open an account, maintain records of the information used to do so, and consult applicable lists of known or suspected terrorists or terrorist organizations. The lists of known or suspected terrorists that the Committee intends financial institutions to consult are those already supplied to financial institutions by the Office of Foreign Asset Control (OFAC), and occasionally by law enforcement and regulatory authorities, as in the days immediately following the September 11, 2001, attacks on the World Trade Center and the Pentagon. It is the Committee's intent that the verification procedures prescribed by Treasury make use of information currently obtained by most financial institutions in the account opening process. It is not the Committee's intent for the regulations to require verification procedures that are prohibitively expensive or impractical.

"Paragraph (3) requires that Treasury consider the various types of accounts maintained by various financial institutions, the various methods of opening accounts, and the various types of identifying information available in promulgating its regulations. This would require Treasury to consider, for example, the feasibility of obtaining particular types of information for accounts opened through the mail, electronically, or in other situations where the accountholder is not physically present at the financial institution. Millions of Americans open accounts at mutual funds, broker-dealers, and other financial institutions in this manner; it is not the Committee's intent that the regulations adopted pursuant to this legislation impose burdens that would make this prohibitively expensive or impractical. This provision allows Treasury to adopt regulations that are appropriately tailored to these types of accounts.

"Current regulatory guidance instructs depository institutions to make reasonable efforts to determine the true identity of all customers requesting an institution's services. (See, e.g., FDIC Division of Supervision Manual of Exam Policies, section 9.4 VI.) The Committee intends that the regulations prescribed under this section adopt a similar approach, and impose requirements appropriate to the size, location, and type of business of an institution.

"Paragraph (4) requires that Treasury consult with the appropriate functional regulator in developing the regulations. This will help ensure that the regulations are appropriately tailored to the business practices of various types of financial institutions, and the risks that such practices may pose.

Federal regulatory authorities must approve the merger of various financial institutions under the Bank Holding Company Act, 12 U.S.C. 1842, and the Federal Deposit Insurance Act, 12 U.S.C. 1828. Section 327 requires consideration of an institution's anti-money laundering record when such mergers are proposed, 12 U.S.C. 1842(c)(6), 1828(c)(11).

Section 314 directs the Secretary of the Treasury to promulgate regulations in order to encourage financial institutions and law enforcement agencies to share information concerning suspected money laundering and terrorist activities, 31 U.S.C. 5311 note.

Section 319(b) requires U.S. financial institutions to respond to bank regulatory authorities' requests for anti-money laundering records (within 120 hours) and to Justice or Treasury Department subpoenas or summons for records concerning foreign deposits (within 7 days), 31 U.S.C. 5318(k). Section 319 also calls for civil penalties of up to $10,000 a day for financial institutions who have failed to terminate correspondent accounts with foreign institutions that have ignored Treasury or Justice Department subpoenas or summons, 31 U.S.C. 5318(k)(3).

Section 352 directs the Secretary of the Treasury to promulgate regulations, in consultation with other appropriate regulatory authorities, requiring financial institutions to maintain anti-money laundering programs which must include at least a compliance officer; an employee training program; the development of internal policies, procedures and controls; and an independent audit feature.[68]

Section 359 subjects money transmitters to the regulations and requirements of the Currency and Foreign Transactions Reporting Act (31 U.S.C. 5311 et seq.) and directs the Secretary of the Treasury to report on the need for additional legislation relating to domestic and international underground banking systems.

Federal law obligates the Administration to develop a national strategy for combating money laundering and related financial crimes, 31 U.S.C. 5341. Section 354 insists that the strategy contain data relating to the funding of international terrorism and efforts to prevent, detect, and prosecute such funding, 31 U.S.C. 5341(b)(12).

Section 364 authorizes the Board of Governors of the Federal Reserve to hire guards to protect members of the Board, as well as the Board's property

"Paragraph (5) gives each functional regulator the authority to exempt, by regulation or order, any financial institution or type of account from the regulations prescribed under paragraph (1).

"Paragraph (6) requires that Treasury's regulations prescribed under paragraph (1) become effective within one year after enactment of this bill").

[68] 31 U.S.C. 5318(h); H.R.Rep.No. 107-250, at 72 (2001).

and personnel and that of any Federal Reserve Bank. The guards may carry firearms and make arrests, 12 U.S.C. 248(q).

Reports to Congress

Section 366 instructs the Secretary of the Treasury to report on methods of improving the compliance of financial institutions with the currency transaction reporting requirements and on the possibility of expanding exemptions to the requirements with an eye to improving the quality of data available for law enforcement purposes and reducing the number of unnecessary filings.[69]

Section 324 instructs the Secretary of the Treasury to report on the execution of authority granted under the International Counter Money Laundering and Related Measures subtitle (III-A) of the Act and to recommend any appropriate related legislation, 31 U.S.C. 5311 note.

International Cooperation

Reflecting concern about the ability of law enforcement officials to trace money transfers to this country from overseas, section 328 instructs the Secretary of the Treasury, Secretary of State and Attorney General to make every effort to encourage other governments to require identification of the originator of international wire transfers.[70]

Section 330 expresses the sense of the Congress that the Administration should seek to negotiate international agreements to enable U.S. law

---

[69]31 U.S.C. 5313 note; H.R.Rep.No. 107-205, at 65 (2001).

[70]H.R.Rep.No. 107-250, at 67 (2001)("This section directs the Secretary of the Treasury, in consultation with the Attorney General and the Secretary of State, to (1) take all reasonable steps to encourage foreign governments to require the inclusion of the name of the originator in wire transfer instructions sent to the U.S. and other countries; and (2) report annually to Congress on Treasury's progress in achieving this objective, and on impediments to instituting a regime in which all appropriate identification about wire transfer recipients is included with wire transfers from their point of origination until disbursement.

"The Committee is concerned that inadequate information on the originator of wire transfers from a number of foreign jurisdictions makes it difficult for both law enforcement and financial institutions to properly understand the source of funds entering the United States in wire transfers. Such a lack of clarity could aid money launderers or terrorists in moving their funds into the United States financial system. Additionally, while arguments have been made that there are technical impediments to requiring that complete addressee information appear on all wire transfers terminating in or passing through the United States, the Committee believes that having such information is technically feasible and would aid both financial institutions in performing due diligence and law enforcement in tracking or seizing money that is the derivative of or would be used in the commission of a crime").

enforcement officials to track the financial activities of foreign terrorist organizations, money launderers and other criminals.

Section 360 authorizes the Secretary of the Treasury to direct the U.S. Executive Directors of the various international financial institutions (*i.e.*, the International Monetary Fund, the International Bank for Reconstruction and Development, the European Bank for Reconstruction and Development, the International Development Association, the International Finance Corporation, the Multilateral Investment Guarantee Agency, the African Development Bank, the African Development Fund, the Asian Development Bank, the Bank for Economic Development and Cooperation in the Middle East and North Africa, and the Inter American Investment Corporation): (1) to support the loan and other benefit efforts on behalf of countries that the President determines have supported our anti-terrorism efforts, and (2) to vote to ensure that funds from those institutions are not used to support terrorism.

Crimes

Federal criminal money laundering statutes punish both concealing the fruits of old offenses and financing new ones. They proscribe financial transactions which:

- involve more than $10,000 derived from one of a list of specified underlying crimes, 18 U.S.C. 1957, or
- are intended to promote any of the designated predicate offenses, or
- are intended to evade taxes, or
- are designed to conceal the proceeds generated by any of the predicate offenses, or
- are crafted to avoid transaction reporting requirements, 18 U.S.C. 1956.

They also condemn transporting funds into, out of, or through the United States with the intent to further a predicate offense, conceal its proceeds, or evade reporting requirements, 18 U.S.C. 1956. Offenders face imprisonment for up to twenty years, fines of up to $500,000, civil penalties, 18 U.S.C. 1956, 1957, and confiscation of the illicit funds involved in a violation or in any of the predicate offenses, 18 U.S.C. 981, 982.

The Act contains a number of new money laundering crimes, as well as amendments and increased penalties for existing crimes. Section 315, for example, adds several crimes to the federal money laundering predicate offense list of 18 U.S.C. 1956. The newly added predicate offenses include crimes in violation of the laws of the other nations when the proceeds are involved in financial transactions in this country: crimes of violence, public corruption, smuggling, and offenses condemned in treaties to which we are a party, 18 U.S.C. 1956(c)(7)(B). Additional federal crimes also join the predicate list:

- 18 U.S.C. 541 (goods falsely classified)
- 18 U.S.C. 922(1) (unlawful importation of firearms)
- 18 U.S.C. 924(n) (firearms trafficking)
- 18 U.S.C. 1030 (computer fraud and abuse)
- felony violations of the Foreign Agents Registration Act, 22 U.S.C. 618.

As the report accompanying H.R. 3004 explains:

> This amendment enlarges the list of foreign crimes that can lead to money laundering prosecutions in this country when the proceeds of additional foreign crimes are laundered in the United States. The additional crimes include all crimes of violence, public corruption, and offenses covered by existing bilateral extradition treaties. The Committee intends this provision to send a strong signal that the United States will not tolerate the use of its financial institutions for the purpose of laundering the proceeds of such activities. H.R.Rep.No. 107-250, at 55 (2000).

In this same vein, section 376 adds the crime of providing material support to a terrorist organization (18 U.S.C. 2339B) to the predicate offense list and section 318 expands 18 U.S.C. 1956 to cover financial transactions conducted in foreign financial institutions.[71]

---

[71]"[S]ection 1956 of title 18, United States Code, makes it an offense to conduct a transaction involving a financial institution if the transaction involves criminally derived property. Similarly, 18 U.S.C. 1957 creates an offense relating to the deposit, withdrawal, transfer or exchange of criminally derived funds 'by, to or through a financial institution.' For the purposes of both statutes, the term 'financial institution' is defined in 31 U.S.C. 5312. See 18 U.S.C. 1956(c)(6); 18 U.S.C. 1957(f).

"The definition of 'financial institution' in 5312 does not explicitly include foreign banks. Such banks may well be covered because they fall within the meaning of 'commercial bank' or other terms in the statute, but as presently drafted, there is some confusion over whether the government can rely on section 5312 to prosecute an offense under either 1956 or 1957 involving a transaction through a foreign bank, even if the offense occurs in part in the United States. For example, if a person in the United States sends criminal proceeds abroad--say to a Mexican bank--and launders them through a series of financial transactions, the government conceivably could not rely on the definition of a 'financial institution' in

Section 329 makes it a federal crime to corruptly administer the money laundering regulatory scheme. Offenders are punishable by imprisonment for not more than 15 years and a fine of not more than three times the amount of the bribe.

Section 5326 of title 31 authorizes the Secretary of the Treasury to impose temporary, enhanced reporting requirements upon financial institutions in areas victimized by substantial money laundering activity (geographic targeting regulations and orders). Section 353 makes it clear that the civil sanctions, criminal penalties, and prohibitions on smurfing (structuring transactions to evade reporting requirements) apply to violations of the regulations and orders issued under 31 U.S.C. 5326.[72] It also extends the permissible length of the temporary geographical orders from 60 to 180 days.

Violations of the special measures and special due diligence requirements of sections 311 and 312 are subject to both civil and criminal penalties by virtue of section 363's amendments to 31 U.S.C. 5321(a) and 5322. The amendments authorize civil penalties and criminal fines of twice the amount of the transaction but not more than $1 million. Criminal offenders would be subject to a fine in the same amount.

Earlier federal law prohibited the operation of illegal money transmitting businesses, 18 U.S.C. 1960. Section 373 amends the proscription to make it clear that the prohibition must be breached "knowingly" and to cover businesses which are otherwise lawful but which transmit funds they know are derived from or intended for illegal activities. It also amends 18 U.S.C. 981(a)(1)(A) to permit civil forfeiture of property involved in a transaction in violation of 18 U.S.C. 1960.[73]

1956(c)(6) to establish that the transaction was a 'financial transaction' within the meaning of 1956(c)(4)(B) (defining a 'financial transaction' as a transaction involving the use of a 'financial institution'), or that it was a 'monetary transaction' within the meaning of 1957(f) (defining 'monetary transaction' as, inter alia, a transaction that would be a 'financial transaction' under 1956(c)(4)(B)).

"Similarly, the money laundering laws in effect in most countries simply make it an offense to launder the proceeds of any crime, foreign or domestic. In the United States, however, the money laundering statute is violated only when a person launders the proceeds of one of the crimes set forth on a list of 'specified unlawful activities.' 18 U.S.C. 1956(c)(7). Currently only a handful of foreign crimes appear on that list. See 1956(c)(7)(B)," H.R.Rep.No. 107-250, at 38 (2000).

[72] *Cf.*, H.R.Rep.No. 107-250, at 57.

[73] "The operation of an unlicensed money transmitting business is a violation of Federal law under 18 U.S.C. 1960. First, section 104 clarifies the scienter requirement in 1960 to avoid the problems that occurred when the Supreme Court interpreted the currency transaction reporting statutes to require proof that the defendant knew that structuring a cash transaction to avoid the reporting requirements had been made a criminal offense. See Ratzlaf v. United States, 114 S. Ct. 655 (1994). The proposal makes clear that an offense under 1960 is a

Sections 374 and 375 of the Act seek to curtail economic terrorism by increasing and making more uniform the penalties for counterfeiting U.S. or foreign currency and by making it clear that the prohibitions against possession of counterfeiting paraphernalia extend to their electronic equivalents.[74] They increase the maximum terms of imprisonment for violation of:

- 18 U.S.C. 471 (obligations or securities of the U.S.) from 15 to 20 years;
- 18 U.S.C. 472 (uttering counterfeit obligations and securities) from 15 to 20 years;
- 18 U.S.C. 473 (dealing in counterfeit obligations and securities) from 10 to 20 years;
- 18 U.S.C. 476 (taking impressions of tools used for obligations and securities) from 10 to 25 years;
- 18 U.S.C. 477 (possessing or selling impressions of tools used for obligations or securities) from 10 to 25 years;
- 18 U.S.C. 484 (connecting parts of different notes) from 5 to 10 years;

general intent crime for which a defendant is liable if he knowingly operates an unlicensed money transmitting business. For purposes of a criminal prosecution, the Government would not have to show that the defendant knew that a State license was required or that the Federal registration requirements promulgated pursuant to 31 U.S.C. 5330 applied to the business.

"Second, section 104 expands the definition of an unlicensed money transmitting business to include a business engaged in the transportation or transmission of funds that the defendant knows are derived from a criminal offense, or are intended to be used for an unlawful purpose. Thus, a person who agrees to transmit or to transport drug proceeds for a drug dealer, or funds from any source for a terrorist, knowing such funds are to be used to commit a terrorist act, would be engaged in the operation of an unlicensed money transmitting business. It would not be necessary for the Government to show that the business was a storefront or other formal business open to walk-in trade. To the contrary, it would be sufficient to show that the defendant offered his services as a money transmitter to another.

"Finally, when Congress enacted 1960 in 1992, it provided for criminal but not civil forfeiture. The proposal corrects this oversight, and allows the government to obtain forfeiture of property involved in the operation of an illegal money transmitting business even if the perpetrator is a fugitive," H.R.Rep.No. 107-250, at 54 (2001).

[74] "This section makes it a criminal offense to possess an electronic image of an obligation or security document of the United States with intent to defraud. The provision harmonizes counterfeiting language to clarify that possessing either analog or digital copies with intent to defraud constitutes an offense. This section mimics existing language that makes it a felony to possess the plates from which currency can be printed, and takes into account the fact that most counterfeit currency seized today is generated by computers or computer-based equipment. The section also increases maximum sentences for a series of counterfeiting offenses," H.R.Rep.No. 107-250, at 75-6 (2001).

- 18 U.S.C. 493 (bonds and obligations of certain lending agencies) from 5 to 10 years;
- 18 U.S.C. 478 (foreign obligations or securities) from 5 to 20 years;
- 18 U.S.C. 479 (uttering counterfeit foreign obligations or securities) from 3 to 20 years;
- 18 U.S.C. 480 (possessing counterfeit foreign obligations or securities) from 1 to 20 years;
- 18 U.S.C. 481 (plates, stones, or analog, digital, or electronic images for counterfeiting foreign obligations or securities) from 5 to 25 years;
- 18 U.S.C. 482 (foreign bank notes) from 2 to 20 years; and
- 18 U.S.C. 483 (uttering counterfeit foreign bank notes) from 1 to 20 years.

Aliens believed to have engaged in money laundering may not enter the United States, section 1006 (8 U.S.C. 1182(a)(2)(I)). The same section directs the Secretary of State to maintain a watchlist to ensure that they are not admitted, 8 U.S.C. 1182 note.

Bulk Cash

Customs officials ask travelers leaving the United States whether they are taking $10,000 or more in cash with them. Section 1001 of title 18 of the United States Code makes a false response punishable by imprisonment for not more than 5 years. Section 5322 of title 31 makes failure to report taking $10,000 or more to or from the United States punishable by the same penalties. The Act's bulk cash smuggling offense, section 371, augments these proscriptions with a somewhat unique feature, 31 U.S.C. 5332 – a criminal forfeiture of the smuggled cash in lieu of a criminal fine. The basic offense outlaws smuggling cash into or out of the United States. The concealment element of the offense seems to cover everything but in-sight possession as long as an amount $10,000 or more is carried in manner to evade reporting.[75]

The section appears to be the product of reactions to the Supreme Court's decision in *United States v. Bajakian*, 524 U.S. 321 (1998). There officials had confiscation $350,000 because Bajakian attempted to leave the country without declaring it, a violation of 31 U.S.C. 5322. In the view of the Court, the confiscation was grossly disproportionate to the gravity of the offense and consequently contrary to the Constitution's excessive fines clause, 524 U.S. at 337. The Committee Report accompanying H.R. 3004 explains the Justice Department's assurance that casting surreptitious removal of cash from the United States as a smuggling rather than a false reporting offense will avoid the adverse consequences of the Supreme Court's examination of forfeiture in false reporting cases under the Constitution's Excessive Fines Clause.[76]

Section 5317 of title 31 once called for civil forfeiture of property traceable to a violation of 31 U.S.C. 5316 (reports on exporting or importing money instruments worth $10,000 or more). Section 372 of the Act recasts section 5317 to provide for civil and criminal forfeitures for violations of 31 U.S.C. 5316, of 31 U.S.C. 5313 (reports on domestic coins and currency transactions involving $10,000 or more) and of 31 U.S.C. 5324 (structuring transactions to evade reporting requirements (smurfing)).

Extraterritorial Jurisdiction

The Act makes 18 U.S.C. 1029, the federal statute condemning various crimes involving credit cards, PIN numbers and other access devices,

---

[75] "For purposes of this section, the concealment of currency on the person of any individual includes concealment in any article of clothing worn by the individual or in any luggage, backpack, or other container worn or carried by such individual," 31 U.S.C. 5332(a)(2).

[76] "As recent Congressional hearings have demonstrated, currency smuggling is an extremely serious law enforcement problem. Hundreds of millions of dollars in U.S. currency – representing the proceeds of drug trafficking and other criminal offenses – is annually transported out of the United States to foreign countries in shipments of bulk cash. Smugglers use all available means to transport the currency out of the country, from false bottoms in personal luggage, to secret compartments in automobiles, to concealment in durable goods exported for sale abroad....

"Presently, the only law enforcement weapon against such smuggling is section 5316 of title 31, United States Code, which makes it an offense to transport more than $10,000 in currency or monetary instruments into, or out of, the United State without filing a report with the United States Customs Service. The effectiveness of section 5316 as a law enforcement tool has been diminished, however, by a recent Supreme Court decision. In *United States v. Bajakajian*, 118 S.Ct. 2028 (1998), the Supreme Court held that section 5316 constitutes a mere reporting violation, which is not a serious offense for purposes of the Excessive Fines Clause of the Eighth Amendment. Accordingly, confiscation of the full amount of the smuggled currency is unconstitutional, even if the smuggler took elaborate steps to conceal the currency and otherwise obstruct justice.

"Confiscation of the smuggled currency is, of course, the most effective weapon that can be employed against currency smugglers. Accordingly, in response to the *Bajakajian* decision, the Department of Justice proposed making the act of bulk cash smuggling itself a criminal offense, and to authorize the imposition of the full range of civil and criminal sanctions when the offense is discovered. Because the act of concealing currency for the purpose of smuggling it out of the United States is inherently more serious than simply failing to file a Customs report, strong and meaningful sanctions, such as confiscation of the smuggled currency, are likely to withstand Eighth Amendment challenges to the new statute," H.R.Rep.No. 107-250 at 36-7 (2001).

applicable overseas if the card or device is issued by or controlled by an American bank or other entity *and* some article is held in or transported to or through the United States during the course of the offense, section 377. The change was part of the original Justice Department proposals. Justice explained that, "[financial crime[] admits of no border, utilizing the integrated global financial network for ill purposes. This provision would apply the financial crimes prohibitions to conduct committed abroad, so long as the tools or proceeds of the crimes pass through or are in the United States," *DoJ* at §408. The section, however, appears to limit the otherwise applicable extraterritorial jurisdiction implicit in section 1029, since federal courts would likely recognize extraterritorial jurisdiction over a violation under *either* circumstance (issued by a U.S. entity or physical presence in the U.S.) as well as a number of others.[77]

Venue

Section 1004 relies on *dicta* in *United States v. Cabrales*, 524 U.S. 1, 8 (1998), in order to permit a money laundering prosecution to be brought in the place where the crime which generated the funds occurred, "if the defendant participated in the transfer of the proceeds," 18 U.S.C. 1956(i).

Ordinarily, the Constitution requires that a crime be prosecuted in the state and district in which it occurs, in the case of money laundering,[78] in the state and district in which the monetary transaction takes place. The Supreme Court in *Cabrales* held that a charge of money laundering in Florida, of the proceeds of a Missouri drug trafficking, could not be tried in Missouri. The Court declared in *dicta*, however, that "money laundering...arguably might rank as a continuing offense, triable in more than one place, if the launderer acquired the funds in one district and transported them into another," 524 U.S. at 8.[79]

---

[77] *United States v. Bowman*, 260 U.S. 94, 97-8 (1922); *Ford v. United States*, 273 U.S. 593, 623 (1927). For a general discussion of the extraterritorial application of federal criminal law, *see*, Doyle, *Extraterritorial Application of American Criminal Law*, CRS REP.NO. 94-166A (Mar. 13, 1999).

[78] "The trial of all crimes...shall be held in the state where the said crimes shall have been committed; but when not committed within any state, the trial shall be at such place or places as the Congress may by law have directed," *U.S.Const.* Art.III, §2, cl.3.

"[I]n all criminal prosecutions, the accused shall enjoy the right to a speedy and public trial, by an impartial jury of the state and district wherein the crime shall have been committed; which district shall have been previously ascertained by law," *U.S.Const.* Amend. VI.

[79] *See also*, *United States v. Rodriguez-Moreno*, 526 U.S. 275, 280-81 n.4 (1999) (holding that acquiring and using a firearm in Maryland in connection with a kidnaping in New Jersey might constitutionally be prosecuted in New Jersey under a statute which outlawed possession of a firearm "during and in relation to" a crime of violence.

Forfeiture

Forfeiture is the government confiscation of property as a consequence of crime.[80] The forfeiture amendments of the Act fall into two categories. Some make adjustments to those portions of federal forfeiture law which govern the confiscation of property derived from, or used to facilitate, various federal crimes. Others follow the pattern used for the war-time confiscation of the property of enemy aliens under the Trading With the Enemy Act, 50 U.S.C.App. 1 *et seq.* (TWEA), forfeitures which turn on the ownership of the property rather than upon its proximity to any particular crime.

Constitutional Considerations

The Act adds TWEA-like amendments to the International Emergency Economic Powers Act (IEEPA), 50 U.S.C. 1701 *et seq.*, which already allowed the President to freeze the assets of foreign terrorists under certain conditions. Under IEEPA, as amended by section 106 of the Act, the President or his delegate may confiscate and dispose of any property, within the jurisdiction of the United States, belonging to any foreign individual, foreign entity, or foreign country whom they determine to have planned, authorized, aided or engaged in an attack on the United States by a foreign country or foreign nationals. The section also permits the government to present secretly (ex parte and in camera) any classified information upon which the forfeiture was based should the decision be subject to judicial review. The Justice Department requested the section as a revival of the President's powers in times of unconventional wars.[81] By virtue of section

[80]For general background information, *see*, Doyle, *Crime and Forfeiture*, CRS REP. NO. 97-139A (Oct. 11, 2000).

[81]"This section is designed to accomplish two principal objectives. First, the section restores to the President, in limited circumstances involving armed hostilities or attacks against the United States, the power to confiscate and vest in the United States property of enemies during times of national emergency, which was contained in the Trading with the Enemy Act, 50 App. U.S.C. §5(b)(TWEA) until 1977. Until the International Economic Emergency Act (IEEPA) was passed in 1977, section 5(b) permitted the President to vest enemy property in the United States during time of war *or* national emergency. When IEEPA was passed, it did not expressly include a provision permitting the vesting of property in the United States, and section 5(b) of TWEA was amended to apply only 'during the time of war.' 50 App.U.S.C. §5(b).

"This new provision tracks the vesting language currently in section 5(b) of TWEA and permits the President, only in the limited circumstances when the United States is engaged in military hostilities or has been subject to an attack, to confiscate property of any foreign country, person, or organization involved in hostilities or attacks on the United States. Like the original provision in TWEA, it is an exercise of Congress's war power under Article I,

316, property owners may initiate a challenge to a confiscation by filing a claim under the rules applicable in maritime confiscations. The section permits two defenses to forfeiture – that the property is not subject to confiscation under section 106 or that the claimant is entitled to the innocent owner defense of 18 U.S.C. 983(d).[82] The characterization of the defenses as "affirmative defense" indicates that the claimant bears the burden of proof. The innocent owner defenses of 18 U.S.C. 983(d) are probably not available in cases under section 106, since that section is explicitly excepted from the coverage of 18 U.S.C. 983.[83] The challenge proceedings permit the court to admit evidence, such as hearsay evidence, that would not otherwise be admissible under the Federal Rules of Evidence if the evidence is reliable and if national security might be imperiled should dictates of the Federal Rules be followed, §316(b). The section recognizes the rights of claimants to proceed alternatively under the Constitution or the Administrative Procedure Act.[84]

The Justice Department also recommended enactment of an overlapping provision which ultimately passed as section 806 of the Act without any real

section 8, clause 11 of the Constitution and is designed to apply to unconventional warfare where Congress has not formally declared war against a foreign nation.

"The second principal purpose of this amendment to IEEPA is to ensure that reviewing courts may base their rulings on an examination of the complete administrative record in sensitive national security or terrorism cases without requiring the United States to compromise classified information. New section (c) would authorize a reviewing court, in the process of verifying that determinations made by the executive branch were based upon substantial evidence and were not arbitrary or capricious, to consider classified evidence ex parte and in camera. This would ensure that reviewing courts have the best and most complete information upon which to base their decisions without forcing the United States to choose between compromising highly sensitive intelligence information or declining to take action against individuals or entities that may present a serious threat to the United States or its nationals. A similar accommodation mechanism was enacted by Congress in the Anti-Terrorism and Effective Death Penalty Act of 1996, 8 U.S.C. §1189(b)(2)," *DoJ* at §159.

[82] "An owner of property that is confiscated under any provision of law relating to the confiscation of assets of suspected international terrorists, may contest that confiscation by filing a claim in the manner set forth in the Federal Rules of Civil Procedure (Supplemental Rules for Certain Admiralty and Maritime Claims), and asserting as an affirmative defense that – (1) the property is not subject to confiscation under such provision of law; or (2) the innocent owner provisions of section 983(d) of title 18, United States Code, apply to the case," Sec. 316(a).

[83] 18 U.S.C. 983(i)(2)(D).

[84] "The exclusion of certain provisions of Federal law from the definition of the term 'civil forfeiture statute' in section 983(i) of title 18, United States Code, shall not be construed to deny an owner of property the right to contest the confiscation of assets of suspected international terrorists under – (A) subsection (a) of this section; (B) the Constitution; or (C) subchapter II of chapter 5 of title 5, United States Code (commonly known as the 'Administrative Procedure Act')," Sec. 316(c)(1).

discussion of the relationship of the two sections.[85] Section 806 authorizes confiscation of all property, regardless of where it is found, of any individual, entity, or organization engaged in domestic or international terrorism (as defined in 18 U.S.C. 2331),[86] against the United States, Americans or their property, 18 U.S.C. 981(a)(1)(G). Section 806 as discussed below also calls for the more common confiscation of property derived from and or facilitating acts of domestic or international terrorism against the United States or its citizens. Confiscations under 806 may be challenged under the procedures of 18 U.S.C. 983, since they are not exempted there. To the extent that forfeiture under section 806 is based on international rather than domestic terrorism, claimants may also use the procedures of section 316.

Confiscation based solely on the fact that the property is owned by a criminal offender, rather than that it is derived from or facilitates some crime is fairly uncommon. It is the mark of common law forfeiture of estate. At common law, a felon forfeited all of his property. Most contemporary

---

[85] "Current law does not contain any authority tailored specifically to the confiscation of terrorist assets. Instead, currently, forfeiture is authorized only in narrow circumstances for the proceeds of murder, arson, and some terrorism offenses, or for laundering the proceeds of such offenses. However, most terrorism offenses do not yield 'proceeds,' and available current forfeiture laws require detailed tracing that is quite difficult for accounts coming through the banks of countries used by many terrorists.

"This section increases the government's ability to strike at terrorist organizations' economic base by permitting the forfeiture of its property regardless of the source of the property, and regardless of whether the property has actually been used to commit a terrorism offense. This is similar in concept to the forfeiture now available under RICO. In parity with the drug forfeiture laws, the section also authorizes the forfeiture of property used or intended to be used to facilitate a terrorist act, regardless of its source. There is no need for a separate criminal forfeiture provision because criminal forfeiture is incorporated under current law by reference. The provision is retroactive to permit it to be applied to the events of September 11, 2001," *DoJ*, at §403. The House Report on H.R. 2975 which contained versions of both sections is no more explicit on the relation of the two sections.

[86] "(1) the term 'international terrorism' means activities that – (A) involve violent acts or acts dangerous to human life that are a violation of the criminal laws of the United States or of any State, or that would be a criminal violation if committed within the jurisdiction of the United States or of any State; (B) appear to be intended – (i) to intimidate or coerce a civilian population; (ii) to influence the policy of a government by intimidation or coercion; or (iii) to affect the conduct of a government by mass destruction, assassination or kidnapping; and (C) occur primarily outside the territorial jurisdiction of the United States, or transcend national boundaries in terms of the means by which they are accomplished, the persons they appear intended to intimidate or coerce, or the locale in which their perpetrators operate or seek asylum...(5) the term 'domestic terrorism' means activities that – (A) involve acts dangerous to human life that are a violation of the criminal laws of the United States or of any State; (B) appear to be intended – (i) to intimidate or coerce a civilian population; (ii) to influence the policy of a government by intimidation or coercion; or (iii) to affect the conduct of a government by mass destruction, assassination or kidnapping; and (C) occur primarily within the territorial jurisdiction of the United States," 18 U.S.C. 2331(1),(5)(as amended by section 802 of the Act).

forfeiture statutes employ statutory forfeiture, a more familiar presence in American law,[87] which consists of the confiscation of things whose possession is criminal, of the fruits of crime, and of the means of crime – untaxed whiskey, the drug dealer's profits, and the rum runner's ship.

Three characteristics set forfeiture of estate apart. The property is lost solely by reason of its ownership by a felon. All of a felon's property is confiscated, not merely that which is related to the crime for which he is convicted. Finally, it occasions attainder which negates the felon's right to hold property or for title to property to pass through him to his heirs. It was with this in mind, that the Framers declared that "no attainder of treason shall work corruption of blood or forfeiture exception during the life of the person attainted."[88] And for this reason, President Lincoln insisted that the confiscated real estate of Confederate supporters should revert their heirs at death.[89]

Neither section 106 nor 806 require conviction of the terrorist property owner.[90] Both call for forfeiture of all of the terrorist's property, without requiring any nexus to the terrorist's offenses other than terrorist ownership. Neither makes any explicit provision for the terrorist's heirs. Section 106 applies only to foreign persons, organizations, or countries, but section 806 recognizes no such distinction.

Of course, the Supreme Court long ago confirmed the constitutional validity of a seemingly similar pattern in TWEA under the President's war powers.[91] The Court was careful to point out, however, that the TWEA

---

[87] *Austin v. United States*, 509 U.S. 602, 611-12 (1993)("Three kinds of forfeiture were established in England at the time the Eighth Amendment was ratified in the United States: deodand, forfeiture, and statutory forfeiture.... Of England's three kinds of forfeiture, only the third took hold in the United States").

[88] *U.S.Const.* Art.III, §3, cl.2.

[89] 12 Stat. 589, 627 (1862). Some would suggest a fourth distinction: that it follows a felony conviction. This is hardly a distinction, since over time legislation creating statutory forfeitures has employed criminal *in personam* proceedings following criminal conviction as a means of accomplishing confiscation.

[90] Although by operation of law property subject to civil forfeiture of section 806 may be confiscated upon conviction of the property owner for any crime of domestic or international terrorism, 28 U.S.C. 2461(c)("If a forfeiture of property is authorized in connection with a violation of an Act of Congress, and any person is charged in an indictment or information with such violation but no specific statutory provision is made for criminal forfeiture upon conviction, the Government may include the forfeiture in the indictment or information in accordance with the Federal Rules of Criminal Procedure, and upon conviction, the court shall order the forfeiture of the property in accordance with the procedures set forth in section 413 of the Controlled Substances Act").

[91] *Silesian American Corp. V. Clark*, 332 U.S. 469 (1947); *cf., Societe Internationale v. Rogers*, 357 U.S. 197, 211 (1958)("this summary power to seize property which is believed to be enemy-owned is rescued from constitutional invalidity under the Due Process and Just

procedure was not really forfeiture or confiscation for the benefit of the United States, but by express statutory provision a liquidation measure to protect the creditors of enemy property owners.[92] Neither section 106 nor 806 are part of TWEA and neither explicitly treats the proceeds of confiscation as a fund for the benefit of creditors. Moreover, broad as the President's war powers may be, they would hardly seem to provide a justification for section 806, which embraces domestic terrorism and is neither limited to foreign offenders nor predicated upon war-like hostilities.

Criminal forfeitures, civil forfeitures with punitive as well as remedial purposes, and civil forfeitures whose effect is so punitive as to negate any presumption of remedial purpose, all raise other constitutional points of interest. The Eighth Amendment's excessive fines clause prohibits criminal forfeitures, and civil forfeitures with at least some punitive purposes, that are grossly disproportionate to the gravity of the crimes which trigger them.[93] The Fifth Amendment's double jeopardy clause applies to criminal forfeitures and civil forfeitures which are so punitive as to negate any presumption of remedial purposes.[94] The same has been said of the applicability of the ex post facto clause.[95]

The limitations on criminal forfeitures would apply to the forfeitures under section 806 when prosecuted as criminal forfeitures by operation of 28 U.S.C. 2461(c). The offenses that activate section 106 and 806 confiscations, however, are of such gravity that successful excessive fine clause challenges are unlikely, even if the value of confiscated property were extraordinarily high.

On the other hand, there is more than a little support for the argument that section 106 and 806 constitute punitive rather than remedial measures.

Compensation Clauses of the Fifth Amendment only by those provisions of the Act which afford a non-enemy claimant a later judicial hearing as to the propriety of the seizure").

[92] *Zittman v. McGrath*, 341 U.S. 471, 473-74 (1951)(citing 50 U.S.C.App. 34) ("While the statute under which the funds are to be 'held, administered and accounted for' authorizes the vesting of such foreign-owned property in the custodian and its administration 'in the interest of and for the benefit of the United States,' it is not a confiscation measure, but a liquidation measure for the protection of American creditors. It provides for the filing and proving of claims and states that the funds 'shall be equitably applied for the payments of debts").

[93] *United States v. Bajakajian*, 524 U.S. 321, 337 (1998); *Austin v. United States*, 509 U.S. 602, 622 (1993).

[94] *United States v. Ursery*, 518 U.S. 267, 278 (1996).

[95] *See e.g., United States v. Certain Funds (Hong Kong and Shanghai Banking Corp.)*, 96 F.3d 20, 26-7 (2d Cir. 1996). Where the ex post facto clauses do not apply, the validity of retroactive statutes is judged by due process clause standards. There is a presumption against retroactive application in such instances absent a clear indication of contrary Congressional intent grounded in the view that due process demands certain minimal notice of the law's demands, *Landgraf v. USI Film Products*, 511 U.S. 244, 265-66 (1994).

They are potentially severe. Section 806 calls for the total impoverishment of those to whom it applies (all assets foreign and domestic), while section 106 anticipates confiscation of all assets within the jurisdiction of the United States. They seem to undermine any claim to remedial purpose by reaching those assets that neither facilitate the commission of terrorism nor constitute its fruits. Moreover, in its analysis of the language of section 806, the Justice Department described it as conceptually akin to the criminal forfeiture provisions of RICO.[96] If the courts find section 106 or 806 are civil in name but criminal in nature, they may well conclude that efforts to enforce the sections are bound by the limitations of the double jeopardy and ex post facto clauses.

Other Forfeiture Amendments

In order to more effectively enforce money laundering penalties and prosecute civil forfeiture actions involving foreign individuals or entities, section 317 of the Act establishes a procedure for long-arm jurisdiction over individuals and entities located overseas and for the appointment of a federal receiver to take control of contested assets during the pendency of the proceedings.[97]

---

[96] *DoJ*, at §403.

[97] 18 U.S.C. 1956(b). *Cf.*, H.R.Rep.No. 107-250, at 54-5 (2001)("The first provision in this section creates a long arm statute that gives the district court jurisdiction over a foreign person, including a foreign bank, that commits a money laundering offense in the United States or converts laundered funds that have been forfeited to the Government to his own use. Thus, if the Government files a civil enforcement action under section 1956(b), or files a civil lawsuit to recover forfeited property from a third party, the district court would have jurisdiction over the defendant if the defendant has been served with process pursuant to the applicable statutes or rules of procedure, and the constitutional requirement of minimum contacts is satisfied in one of three ways: the money laundering offense took place in the United States; in the case of converted property, the property was the property of the United States by virtue of a civil or criminal forfeiture judgment; or in the case of a financial institution, the defendant maintained a correspondent bank account at another bank in the United States. Under this provision, for example, the district courts would have had jurisdiction over the defendant in the circumstances described in United States v. Swiss American Bank, 191 F.3d 30 (1st Cir. 1999).

"The second provision, modeled on 18 U.S.C. 1345(b), gives the district court the power to restrain property, issue seizure warrants, or take other action necessary to ensure that a defendant in an action covered by the statute does not dissipate the assets that would be needed to satisfy a judgment.

"This section also authorizes a court, on the motion of the Government or a State or Federal regulator, to appoint a receiver to gather and protect assets needed to satisfy a judgment under sections 1956 and 957, and the forfeiture provisions in sections 981 and 982. This authority is intended to apply in three circumstances: (1) when there is a judgment in a criminal case, including an order of restitution, following a conviction for a violation of section 1956 or 1957; (2) when there is a judgment in a civil case under section 1956(b) assessing a penalty for a violation of either section 1956 or 1957; and (3) when there is a

In the case of interbank accounts where a bank in a foreign nation has an account in a bank located in the United States, section 319(a) allows seizure of funds in an account here when the foreign bank has received money laundering or drug trafficking deposits overseas.[98] Confiscation proceedings are conducted pursuant to 18 U.S.C. 953.

Federal law has for some time permitted criminal forfeiture orders to reach substitute assets if the property of the defendant subject to confiscation has become unavailable. Section 319(d) establishes a procedure under which a convicted defendant may be ordered to transfer property to this country from overseas if the property is subject to confiscation.[99]

---

civil forfeiture judgment under section 981 or a criminal forfeiture judgment, including a personal money judgment, under section 982.

"The amendment also makes section 1956(b) applicable to violations of section 1957. It applies to conduct occurring before the effective date of the Act").

[98] 18 U.S.C. 981(k). H.R.Rep.No. 107-250, at 57-8 (2001)("Section 114 creates a new provision in the civil forfeiture statute, 18 U.S.C. 981(k), authorizing the forfeiture of funds found in an interbank account. The new provision is necessary to reconcile the law regarding the forfeiture of funds in bank accounts with the realities of the global movement of electronic funds and the use of off-shore banks to insulate criminal proceeds from forfeiture. 'To prevent drug dealers and other criminals from taking advantage of certain nuances of forfeiture law to insulate their property from forfeiture even though it is deposited in a bank account in the United States, it is necessary to change the law regarding the location of the debt that a bank owes to its depositor, and the identity of the real party in interest with standing to contest the forfeiture. The amendment in this section addresses the location issue by treating a deposit made into an account in a foreign bank that has a correspondent account at a U.S. bank as if the deposit had been made into the U.S. bank directly. Second, the section treats the deposit in the correspondent account as a debt owed directly to the depositor, and not as a debt owed to the respondent bank. In other words, the correspondent account is treated as if it were the foreign bank itself, and the funds in the correspondent account were debts owed to the foreign bank's customers.

"Under this arrangement, if funds traceable to criminal activity are deposited into a foreign bank, the Government may bring a forfeiture action against funds in that bank's correspondent account, and only the initial depositor, and not the intermediary bank, would have standing to contest it.

"The section authorizes the Attorney General to suspend or terminate a forfeiture in cases where there exists a conflict of laws between the U.S. and the jurisdiction in which the foreign bank is located, where such suspension or termination would be in the interest of justice and not harm U.S. national interests").

[99] *Cf.*, H.R.Rep.No. 107-250, at 58-9 (2001) ("Section 116 authorizes a court to order a criminal defendant to repatriate his property to the United States in criminal cases. In criminal forfeiture cases, the sentencing court is authorized to order the forfeiture of 'substitute assets' when the defendant has placed the property otherwise subject to forfeiture 'beyond the jurisdiction of the court.' Frequently, this provision is applied when a defendant has transferred drug proceeds or other criminally derived property to a foreign country. In many cases, however, the defendant has no other assets in the United States of a value commensurate with the forfeitable property overseas. In such cases, ordering the forfeiture of substitute assets is a hollow sanction.

"This section amends 21 U.S.C. 853 to make clear that a court in a criminal case may issue a repatriation order--either post-trial as part of the criminal sentence and judgment, or pre-trial pursuant to the court's authority under 21 U.S.C. 853(e) to restrain property--so that they

Prior to enactment of the Act, federal law permitted confiscation of any property in the United States that could be traced to a drug offense committed overseas, if the offense was punishable as a felony under the laws of the nation where it occurred and if the offense would have been a felony if committed here.[100] Section 320 enlarges this provisions to cover not only drug offenses but any of the crimes in the money laundering predicate offense list of 18 U.S.C. 1956(c)(7)(B), and continues the reciprocal felony requirements.[101] This treatment is comparable to the early coverage of the federal statute, 28 U.S.C. 2467, which permitted enforcement of foreign confiscation orders in the case of drug offenses or the crimes on the money laundering predicate offense list. Section 323 of the Act amends the foreign forfeiture enforcement statute to (1) expand the grounds for enforcement to include any crime which would have provided the grounds for confiscation had the offense been committed in the United States; (2) to authorize restraining orders to freeze the target property while enforcement litigation is pending; and (3) to limit the absence-of-timely-notice defense.[102]

---

will be available for forfeiture. Failure to comply with such an order would be punishable as a contempt of court, or it could result in a sentencing enhancement, such as a longer prison term, under the U.S. Sentencing Guidelines, or both").

[100] 18 U.S.C. 981(a)(1)(B).

[101] H.R.Rep.No. 107-250, at 56 (2001)("This section is intended to reinforce the United States' compliance with the Vienna Convention. It amends 18 U.S.C. 981(a)(1)(B) to allow the United States to institute its own action against the proceeds of foreign criminal offenses when such proceeds are found in the United States. As required by the Vienna Convention, it also authorizes the confiscation of property used to facilitate such crimes. The list of foreign crimes to which this section applies is determined by cross-reference to the foreign crimes that are money laundering predicates under 1956(c)(7)(B). This section will permit the forfeiture of property involved in conduct occurring before the effective date of the Act").

[102] H.R.Rep.No. 107–250, at 59–60 (2001)("Under current law, 28 U.S.C. 2467(d) gives Federal courts the authority to enforce civil and criminal forfeiture judgments entered by foreign courts. This section amends that provision to include a mechanism for preserving property subject to forfeiture in a foreign country.

"Specifically, a Federal court could issue a restraining order under 18 U.S.C. 983(j) or register and enforce a foreign restraining order, if the Attorney General certified that such foreign order was obtained in accordance with the principles of due process. A person seeking to contest the restraining order could do so on the ground that 28 U.S.C. 2467 was not properly applied to the particular case, but could not oppose the restraining order on any ground that could also be raised in the proceedings pending in a foreign court. This provision prevents litigant from taking 'two bites at the apple' by raising objections to the basis for the forfeiture in the Federal court that he also raised, or is entitled to raise, in the foreign court where the forfeiture action is pending. It complements the existing provision in section 2467 (e) providing that the Federal court is bound by the findings of fact of the foreign court, and may not look behind such findings in determining whether to enter an order enforcing a foreign forfeiture judgment.

"This section also amends 28 U.S.C. 2467 to make clear that it is not necessary to prove that the person asserting an interest in the property received actual notice of the forfeiture proceedings. As is the case with respect to forfeitures under U.S. Law, it is sufficient if the foreign nation takes steps to provide notice, in accordance with the principles of due process.

A fugitive may not challenge a federal forfeiture.[103] Section 322 applies this fugitive disentitlement to corporations whose major shareholder is a fugitive or whose representative in the confiscation proceedings is a fugitive.

Section 906 instructs the Attorney General, the Secretary of the Treasury, and the Director of Central Intelligence to submit a joint report with recommendations relating to the reconfiguration of the Foreign Terrorist Asset Tracking Center, the Office of Foreign Assets Control, and possibly FinCEN in "order to establish a capability to provide for the effective and efficient analysis and dissemination of foreign intelligence relating to the financial capabilities and resources of international terrorist organizations."

ALIEN TERRORISTS AND VICTIMS

The Act contains a number of provisions designed to prevent alien terrorists from entering the United States, particularly from Canada; to enable authorities to detain and deport alien terrorists and those who support them; and to provide humanitarian immigration relief for foreign victims of the attacks on September 11.

See Gonzalez v. United States, 1997 WL 278123 (S.D.N.Y. 1997)('the [G]overnment is not required to ensure actual receipt of notice that is properly mailed'); Albajon v. Gugliotta, 72 F. Supp. 2d 1362 (S.D. Fla. 1999) (notice sent to various addresses on claimant's identifications, and mailed after claimant released from jail, is sufficient to satisfy due process, even if claimant never received notice); United States v. Schiavo, 897 F. Supp. 644, 648 49 (D. Mass. 1995) (sending notice to fugitive's last known address is sufficient; due process satisfied even if the did not receive the notice).

"Finally, 28 U.S.C. 2467 is amended to authorize the enforcement of a forfeiture judgment based on any foreign offense that would constitute an offense giving rise to a civil or criminal forfeiture of the same property if the offense had been committed in the United States. This is one of two safe guards that the statute contains against the enforcement of judgment that the United States does not consider appropriate for enforcement: if the judgment is based on an act that would not constitute a crime in the United States, such as removing assets from the reach of a repressive regime, it could not be enforced. In addition, section 2467 already provides that a foreign judgment may only be enforced by a Federal court at the request of the United States, and only after the Attorney General has certified that the judgment was obtained in accordance with the principles of due process. Thus, neither a foreign Government nor a foreign private party could enforce a foreign judgment on its own under this provision.)". Note that the safeguard to which the report refers is the range of foreign offenses that will support an enforceable confiscation order, *i,e.,* drug offenses and crimes on the money laundering predicate offense list, and that the amendment narrows that safeguard by adding additional foreign offenses, *i.e.,* any foreign equivalent of a federal crime which would support a confiscation order.

[103] 28 U.S.C. 2466.

Border Protection

The border protection provisions:

- authorize the appropriations necessary to triple the number of Border Patrol, Customs Service, and Immigration and Naturalization Service (INS) personnel stationed along the Northern Border, section 401
- authorize appropriations of an additional $50 million for both INS and the Customs Service to upgrade their border surveillance equipment, section 402
- remove for fiscal year 2001 the $30,000 ceiling on INS overtime pay for border duty, section 404
- authorize appropriations of $2 million for a report to be prepared by the Attorney General on the feasibility of enhancing the FBI's Integrated Automated Fingerprint Identification System (IAFIS) and similar systems to improve the reliability of visa applicant screening, section 405
- authorize the appropriations necessary to provide the State Department and INS with criminal record identification information relating to visa applicants and other applicants for admission to the United States, section 403.
- instruct the Attorney General to report on the feasibility of the use of a biometric identifier scanning system with access to IAFIS for overseas consular posts and points of entry into the United States, section 1007
- direct the Secretary of State to determine whether consular shopping is a problem, to take any necessary corrective action, and to report the action taken, section 418
- express the sense of the Congress that the Administration should implement the integrated entry and exit data system called for by the Illegal Immigration Reform and Immigrant Responsibility Act of 1996 (8 U.S.C. 1365a), section 414
- add the White House Office of Homeland Security to the Integrated Entry and Exit Data System Task Force (8 U.S.C. 1365a note), section 415
- call for the implementation and expansion of the foreign student visa monitoring program (8 U.S.C. 1372), section 416

- limit countries eligible to participate in the visa waiver program to those with machine-readable passports as of October 1, 2003 (8 U.S.C. 1187(c)), section 417
- instruct the Attorney General to report on the feasibility of using biometric scanners to help prevent terrorists and other foreign criminals from entering the country, section 1008[104]
- authorize appropriations of $250,000 for the FBI to determine the feasibility of providing airlines with computer access to the names of suspected terrorists, section 1009
- authorize reciprocal sharing of the State Department's visa lookout data and related information with other nations in order to prevent terrorism, drug trafficking, slave marketing, and gun running, section 413

Detention and Removal

Foreign nationals (aliens) are deportable from the United States, among other grounds, if they were inadmissible at the time they entered the country or if they have subsequently engaged in terrorist activity, 8 U.S.C. 1227 (a)(1)(A), (a)(4)(B), 1182(a)(3)(B)(iv). Aliens may be inadmissible for any number of terrorism-related reasons, 8 U.S.C. 1182 (a)(3)(B). Section 411 of the Act adds to the terrorism-related grounds upon which an alien may be denied admission into the United States and consequently upon which he or she may be deported.

Prior law recognized five terrorism-related categories of inadmissibility. Section 411 redefines two of these – engaging in terrorist activity and representing a terrorist organization (8 U.S.C. 1182(a)(3)(B)(iv), (a)(3)(B)(i)(IV)) – and it adds three more – espousing terrorist activity, being the spouse or child of an inadmissible alien associated with a terrorist organization, and intending to engage in activities that could endanger the welfare, safety or security of the United States (8 U.S.C. 1182(a)(3)(B)(i)(VI), (a)(3)(B)(i)(VII), 1182(a)(3)(F)). It defined engaging in terrorist activity, which is grounds for both inadmissibility and

[104]As the House Judiciary Committee explained, "A biometric fingerprint scanning system is a sophisticated computer scanning technology that analyzes a person's fingerprint and compares the measurement with a verified sample digitally stored in the system. The accuracy of these systems is claimed to be above 99.9%. The biometric identifier system contemplated by this section would have access to the database of the Federal Bureau of Investigation Integrated Automated Fingerprint Identification System," H.R.Rep.No. 107-236, at 78 (2001).

deportation, to encompass soliciting on behalf of a terrorist organization or providing material support to a terrorist organization, 8 U.S.C. 1182(a)(3)(B)(iii)(2000 ed.). It did not explain in so many words, however, what constituted a "terrorist organization," but it presumably included groups designated as terrorist organizations under section 219 of the Immigration and Nationality Act, 8 U.S.C. 1189.

Section 411 defines "terrorist organization" to include not only organizations designated under section 219 but also organizations which the Secretary of State has identified in the *Federal Register* as having provided material support for, committed, incited, planned, or gathered information on potential targets of, terrorist acts of violence, 8 U.S.C. 1182(a)(3)(B)(vi), (a)(3)(B)(iv). It then recasts the definition of engaging in terrorist activities to include solicitation on behalf of such organizations, or recruiting on their behalf, or providing them with material support, 8 U.S.C. 1182(a)(3)(B)(iv). Nevertheless, section 411 permits the Secretary of State or Attorney General to conclude that the material support prohibition does not apply to particular aliens, 8 U.S.C. 1182(a)(3)(B)(vi).

Prior law made representatives of terrorist organizations designated by the Secretary under section 219 (8 U.S.C. 1189) inadmissible, 8 U.S.C. 1182(a)(3)(B)(i)(IV)(2000 ed.). And so they remain. Section 411 makes representatives of political, social or similar groups, whose public endorsements of terrorist activities undermines U.S. efforts to reduce or eliminate terrorism, inadmissible as well, 8 U.S.C.1882(a)(3) (B)(i)(IV).

An individual who uses his or her place of prominence to endorse, espouse, or advocate support for terrorist activities or terrorist organizations in a manner which the Secretary of State concludes undermines our efforts to reduce or eliminate terrorism becomes inadmissible under section 411, 8 U.S.C. 1182(a)(3)(B)(i)(VI).

The spouse or child of an alien, who is inadmissible on terrorist grounds for activity occurring within the last 5 years, is likewise inadmissible, unless the child or spouse was reasonably unaware of the disqualifying conduct or has repudiated the disqualifying conduct, 8 U.S.C. 1182(a)(3)(B)(i)(VII), 1182(a)(3)(B)(ii).

Finally, any alien, whom the Secretary of State or the Attorney General conclude has associated with a terrorist organization and intends to engage in conduct dangerous to the welfare, safety, security of the United States while in this country, is inadmissible, 8 U.S.C. 1182(a)(3)(F).

Section 219 of the Immigration and Nationality Act (8 U.S.C. 1189) permits the Secretary to designate as terrorist organizations any foreign group which he finds to have engaged in terrorist activities. A second subsection 411(c) permits him to designate groups which as subnational groups or clandestine agents, engage in "premeditated, politically motivated violence perpetrated against noncombatant targets," or groups which retain the capacity and intent to engage in terrorism or terrorist activity, 8 U.S.C. 1189(a)(1)(B).

Section 412 permits the Attorney General to detain alien terrorist suspects for up to seven days, 8 U.S.C. 1226a. He must certify that he has reasonable grounds to believe that the suspects either are engaged in conduct which threatens the national security of the United States or are inadmissible or deportable on grounds of terrorism, espionage, sabotage, or sedition. Within seven days, the Attorney General must initiate removal or criminal proceedings or release the alien. If the alien is held, the determination must be reexamined every six months to confirm that the alien's release would threaten national security or endanger some individual or the general public. The Attorney General's determinations are subject to review only under writs of habeas corpus issued out of any federal district court but appealable only to the United States Court of Appeals for the District Columbia. The Attorney General must report to the Judiciary Committee on the details of the operation of section 412.

Uncertain is the relationship between section 412 and the President's Military Order of November 13, 2001, which allows the Secretary of Defense to detain designated alien terrorist suspects, within the United States or elsewhere, without express limitation or condition except with regard to food, water, shelter, clothing, medical treatment, religious exercise, and a proscription on invidious discrimination, 66 *Fed.Reg*. 57833, 57834 (Nov. 16, 2001).

Victims

The Act contains a number of provisions designed to provide immigration relief for foreign nationals, victimized by the attacks of September 11. It provides for:

- permanent resident alien status for eligible aliens and members of their family who but for the events of September 11 would have been eligible for employer-sponsored permanent resident alien status, section 421[105]

[105] "The Act provides permanent resident status through the special immigrant program to an alien who was the beneficiary of a petition filed (on or before September 11) to grant the

- extended filing deadlines for aliens prevented from taking timely action because of immigration office closures, airline schedule disruptions or other similar impediments, section 422[106]

---

alien permanent residence as an employer-sponsored immigrant or of an application for labor certification (filed on or before September 11), if the petition or application was rendered null because of the disability of the beneficiary or loss of employment of the beneficiary due to physical damage to, or destruction of, the business of the petitioner or applicant as a direct result of the terrorist attacks on September 11, or because of the death of the petitioner or applicant as a direct result of the terrorist attacks. Permanent residence would be granted to an alien who was the spouse or child of an alien who was the beneficiary of a petition filed on or before September 11 to grant the beneficiary permanent residence as a family-sponsored immigrant (as long as the spouse or child follows to join not later than September 11, 2003). Permanent residence would be granted to the beneficiary of a petition for a nonimmigrant visa as the spouse or the fiancé (and their children) of a U.S. citizen where the petitioning citizen died as a direct result of the terrorist attack. The section also provides permanent resident status to the grandparents of a child both of whose parents died as a result of the terrorist attacks, if either of such deceased parents was a citizen of the U.S. or a permanent resident," H.R.Rep.No. 107-236, at 66-7 (2001).

[106] "The Act provides that an alien who was legally in a nonimmigrant status and was disabled as a direct result of the terrorist attacks on September 11 (and his or her spouse and children) may remain lawfully in the U.S. (and receive work authorization) until the later of the date that his or her status normally terminates or September 11, 2002. Such status is also provided to the nonimmigrant spouse and children of an alien who died as a direct result of the terrorist attacks.

"The Act provides that an alien who was lawfully present as a nonimmigrant at the time of the terrorist attacks will be granted 60 additional days to file an application for extension or change of status if the alien was prevented from so filing as a direct result of the terrorist attacks. Also, an alien who was lawfully present as a nonimmigrant at the time of the attacks but was then unable to timely depart the U.S. as a direct result of the attacks will be considered to have departed legally if doing so before November 11. An alien who was in lawful nonimmigrant status at the time of the attacks (and his or her spouse and children) but not in the U.S. at that time and was then prevented from returning to the U.S. in order to file a timely application for an extension of status as a direct result of the terrorist attacks will be given 60 additional days to file an application and will have his or her status extended 60 days beyond the original due date of the application.

"Under current law, winners of the fiscal year 2001 diversity visa lottery must enter the U.S. or adjust status by September 30, 2001. The Act provides that such an alien may enter the U.S. or adjust status until April 1, 2002, if the alien was prevented from doing so by September 30, 2001 as a direct result of the terrorist attacks. If the visa quota for the 2001 diversity visa program has already been exceeded, the alien shall be counted under the 2002 program. Also, if a winner of the 2001 lottery died as a direct result of the terrorist attacks, the spouse and children of the alien shall still be eligible for permanent residence under the program. The ceiling placed on the number of diversity immigrants shall not be exceeded in any case.

"Under the Act, in the case of an alien who was issued an immigrant visa that expires before December 31, 2001, if the alien was unable to timely enter the U.S. as a direct result of the terrorist attacks, the validity shall be extended until December 31.

"Under the Act, in the case of an alien who was granted parole that expired on or after September 11, if the alien was unable to enter the U.S. prior to the expiration date as a direct result of the terrorist attacks, the parole is extended an additional 90 days.

"Under the Act, in the case of an alien granted voluntary departure that expired between September 11 and October 11, 2001, voluntary departure is extended an additional 30 days," H.R.Rep.No. 107-236, at 67-8 (2001).

- preservation of certain immigration benefits available to alien family members that would be otherwise lost as a consequence of the death of a victim of September 11, section 423[107]
- limited easing of age restrictions on visas available to aliens under 21 years of age for those whose 21st birthday occurred immediately before or soon after September 11, section 424[108]
- temporary administrative relief for alien family members of a victim of September 11 who are not otherwise entitled to relief under the Act, section 425
- a denial of benefits of the Act to terrorists and their families, section 427
- authority for the Attorney General to establish evidentiary standards to implement the alien victim provisions of the Act, section 426.

OTHER CRIMES, PENALTIES, & PROCEDURES

New Crimes

The Act creates new federal crimes for terrorist attacks on mass transportation facilities, for biological weapons offenses, for harboring terrorists, for affording terrorists material support, for misconduct associated

[107] "Current law provides that an alien who was the spouse of a U.S. citizen for at least 2 years before the citizen died shall remain eligible for immigrant status as an immediate relative. This also applies to the children of the alien. The Act provides that if the citizen died as a direct result of the terrorist attacks, the 2 year requirement is waived.

"The Act provides that if an alien spouse, child, or unmarried adult son or daughter had been the beneficiary of an immigrant visa petition filed by a permanent resident who died as a direct result of the terrorist attacks, the alien will still be eligible for permanent residence. In addition, if an alien spouse, child, or unmarried adult son or daughter of a permanent resident who died as a direct result of the terrorist attacks was present in the U.S. on September 11 but had not yet been petitioned for permanent residence, the alien can self-petition for permanent residence.

"The Act provides that an alien spouse or child of an alien who 1) died as a direct result of the terrorist attacks and 2) was a permanent resident (petitioned-for by an employer) or an applicant for adjustment of status for an employment-based immigrant visa, may have his or her application for adjustment adjudicated despite the death (if the application was filed prior to the death)," H.R.Rep.No. 107-236, at 68 (2001).

[108] "Under current law, certain visas are only available to an alien until the alien's 21st birthday. The Act provides that an alien whose 21st birthday occurs this September and who is a beneficiary for a petition or application filed on or before September 11 shall be considered to remain a child for 90 days after the alien's 21st birthday. For an alien whose 21st birthday occurs after this September, (and who had a petition for application filed on his or her behalf on or before September 11) the alien shall be considered to remain a child for 45 days after the alien's 21st birthday," H.R.Rep.No. 107-236, at 68 (2001).

with money laundering already mentioned, for conducting the affairs of an enterprise which affects interstate or foreign commerce through patterned commission of terrorist offenses, and for fraudulent charitable solicitation. Although strictly speaking these are new federal crimes, they generally supplement existing law filling gaps and increasing penalties.

Pre-existing federal law criminalized, among other things, wrecking trains, 18 U.S.C. 1992, damaging commercial motor vehicles or their facilities, 18 U.S.C. 33, or threatening to do so, 18 U.S.C. 35, destroying vessels within the navigable waters of the United States, 18 U.S.C. 2273, destruction of vehicles or other property used in or used in activities affecting interstate or foreign commerce by fire or explosives, 18 U.S.C. 844(i), possession of a biological agent or toxin as a weapon or a threat, attempt, or conspiracy to do so, 18 U.S.C. 175, use of a weapon of mass destruction affecting interstate or foreign commerce or a threat, attempt, or conspiracy to do so, 18 U.S.C. 2332a, commission of a federal crime of violence while armed with a firearm, or of federal felony while in possession of an explosive, 18 U.S.C. 924(c), 844(h), conspiracy to commit a federal crime, 18 U.S.C. 371.

The Act outlaws terrorist attacks and other actions of violence against mass transportation systems. Offenders may be imprisoned for life or any term of years, if the conveyance is occupied at the time of the offense, or imprisoned for not more than twenty years in other cases, section 801. Under its provisions, it is a crime to willfully:

- wreck, derail, burn, or disable mass transit;
- place a biological agent or destructive device on mass transit recklessly or with the intent to endanger;
- burn or place a biological agent or destructive device in or near a mass transit facility knowing a conveyance is likely to be disabled;
- impair a mass transit signal system;
- interfere with a mass transit dispatcher, operator, or maintenance personnel in the performance of their duties recklessly or with the intent to endanger;
- act with the intent to kill or seriously injure someone on mass transit property;
- convey a false alarm concerning violations of the section;
- attempt to violate the section;
- threaten or conspire to violate the section

when the violation involves interstate travel, communication, or transportation of materials or that involves a carrier engaged in or affecting interstate or foreign commerce, 18 U.S.C. 1993.

Prior to enactment of the Act, federal law proscribed the use of biological agents or toxins as weapons, 18 U.S.C. 175. As suggested by the Justice Department,[109] the Act, in section 817, makes two substantial changes. It makes it a federal offense, punishable by imprisonment for not more than ten years and/or a fine of not more than $250,000, to possess a type or quantity of biological material that cannot be justified for peaceful purposes, 18 U.S.C. 175(b). Second, consistent with federal prohibitions on the possession of firearms, 18 U.S.C. 922(g), and explosives, 18 U.S.C. 842(i), it makes it a federal offenses for certain individuals – such as convicted felons, illegal aliens, and fugitives – to possess biological toxins or agents, 18 U.S.C. 175b.[110] Offenders face the same sanctions, imprisonment for not more than ten years and/or a fine of not more than $250,000.

It is a federal crime to harbor aliens, 8 U.S.C. 1324, or those engaged in espionage, 18 U.S.C. 792; or to commit misprision of a felony (which may take the form of harboring the felon), 18 U.S.C. 4; or to act as an accessory after the fact to a federal crime (including by harboring the offender), 18 U.S.C. 3. The Justice Department had asked that a terrorist harboring offense be added to the espionage section. It also recommended venue and extraterritorial auxiliaries.[111]

---

[109]"Current law prohibits the possession, development, acquisition, etc. of biological agents or toxins for use as a weapon. 18 U.S.C. §175. This section amends the definition of 'for use as a weapon' to include all situations in which it can be proven that the defendant had a purpose other than a prophylactic, protective, or peaceful purpose. This will enhance the government's ability to prosecute suspected terrorists in possession of biological agents or toxins, and conform the scope of the criminal offense in 18 U.S.C. §175 more closely to the related forfeiture provision in 18 U.S.C. §176 [which permits confiscations in cases where the amounts possessed exceed the quantities justifiable for peaceful purposes]. Moreover, the section adds a subsection to 18 U.S.C. §175 which defines an additional offense of possessing a biological agent or toxin of a type or in a quantity that, under the circumstances, is not reasonably justified by a prophylactic, protective or other peaceful purpose. This section also enacts a new statute, 18 U.S.C. 175b, which generally makes it an offense for a person to possess a listed biological agent or toxin if the person is disqualified from firearms possession under 18 U.S.C. §922(g)..." *DoJ* at §305.

[110]The section covers those under felony indictment, those convicted of a felony, fugitives, drug addicts, illegal aliens, mental defectives, aliens from countries which support terrorism, and those dishonorably discharged from the U.S. armed forces, 18 U.S.C. 175b(b)(2).

[111]"18 U.S.C. §792 makes it an offense to harbor or conceal persons engaged in espionage. There is no comparable provision for terrorism, though the harboring of terrorists creates a risk to the nation readily comparable to that posed by harboring spies. This section accordingly amends 18 U.S.C. §792 to make the same prohibition apply to harboring or concealing persons engaged in federal terrorism offenses as defined in section 309 of the bill," *DoJ* at §307; *Draft* at §307(2)("There is extraterritorial Federal jurisdiction over any

The Act, in section 803, instead establishes a separate offense which punishes harboring terrorists by imprisonment for not more than ten years and/or a fine of not more than $250,000, 18 U.S.C. 2339. The predicate offense list consists of:

- destruction of aircraft or their facilities, 18 U.S.C. 32;
- biological weapons offenses, 18 U.S.C. 175;
- chemical weapons offenses, 18 U.S.C. 229;
- nuclear weapons offenses, 18 U.S.C. 831;
- bombing federal buildings, 18 U.S.C. 844(f);
- destruction of an energy facility, 18 U.S.C. 1366;
- violence committed against maritime navigational facilities, 18 U.S.C. 2280;
- offenses involving weapons of mass destruction, 18 U.S.C. 2232a;
- international terrorism, 18 U.S.C. 2232b;
- sabotage of a nuclear facility, 42 U.S.C. 2284;
- air piracy, 49 U.S.C. 46502.

It grants the Justice Department request to permit prosecution either in the place where the harboring occurred or where the underlying act of terrorism committed by the sheltered terrorist might be prosecuted. The Constitution, however, may insist that prosecution take place where the crime of harboring occurred.[112]

---

violation (including, without limitation, conspiracy or attempt) of this section. A violation of this section may be prosecuted in any Federal judicial district in which the underlying offense was committed, or in Federal judicial district as provided by law").

[112] *U.S.Const*. Art.III, §2, cl.3 ("The trial of all crimes...shall be held in the state where the said crimes shall have been committed...."); Amend. IV ("In all criminal prosecutions, the accused shall enjoy the right to a speedy and public trial, by an impartial jury of the state and district wherein the crime shall have been committed...."); *United States v. Cabrales*, 524 U.S. 1 (1998)(a defendant charged with one count of conspiracy to launder the proceeds of a Missouri drug operation and two counts of laundering in Florida could not be prosecuted in Missouri on the laundering counts). The Court might be thought to have retreated somewhat from *Cabrales* when it later approved prosecution for carrying a firearm in relation to a crime of violence in federal court in New Jersey (where the underlying kidnaping occurred) notwithstanding the fact that the firearm had been acquired in Maryland after the defendants left New Jersey with their victim in tow, *United States v. Rodriguez-Moreno*, 526 U.S. 275, 280-81 n.4 (1999)("By way of comparison, last Term in [*Cabrales*] we considered whether venue for money laundering, in violation of 18 U.S.C. 1956(a)(1)(B) (ii) and 1957, was proper in Missouri, where the laundered proceeds were unlawfully generated, or rather, only in Florida, where the prohibited laundering transactions occurred. As we interpreted the laundering statutes at issue, they did not proscribe the anterior criminal conduct that yielded the funds allegedly laundered. The existence of criminally generated proceeds was a circumstance element of the offense but the proscribed conduct – defendant's money

Sections 2339A and 2339B of the title 18 of the United States Code ban providing material support to individuals and to organizations that commit various crimes of terrorism. The Act amends the sections in several ways in section 805. Section 2339B (support of a terrorist organization) joins section 2339A (support of a terrorist) as a money laundering predicate offense, 18 U.S.C. 1956(c)(7)(D) The predicate offense list of 18 U.S.C. 2339A (support to terrorists) grows to include:

- chemical weapons offenses, 18 U.S.C. 229;
- terrorist attacks on mass transportation, 18 U.S.C. 1993;
- sabotage of a nuclear facility, 42 U.S.C. 2284; and
- sabotage of interstate pipelines, 49 U.S.C. 60123(b).

And it adds expert advice or assistance to the types of assistance that may not be provided under section 2339A. This last addition may encounter the same First Amendment vagueness problems some courts have found in assistance which takes the form of "training" and "personnel," *Humanitarian Law Project v. Reno*, 205 F.3d 1130, 1137-136 (9th Cir. 2000).[113] Finally, the section announces that a prosecution for violation of section 2339A (support of terrorists) may be brought where the support is provided or where the predicate act of terrorism occurs. There may be some question whether the Constitution permits prosecution where the predicate act occurs.[114]

Section 813 of the Act also accepts the Justice Department's suggestion that various terrorism offenses be added to the predicate offense list for RICO (racketeer influenced and corrupt organizations) which proscribes

laundering activity – occurred after the fact of an offense begun and completed by others. Here, by contrast, given the 'during and in relation to' language [of section 924], the underlying crime of violence is a critical part of the §924(c)(1) offense").

[113]The Justice Department sought the expansion along with the enlargement of the predicate offense list, "18 U.S.C. §2339A prohibits providing material support or resources to terrorists. The existing definition of 'material support or resources' is generally not broad enough to encompass expert services and assistance – for example, advice provided by a person with expertise in aviation matters to facilitate an aircraft hijacking, or advice provided by an accountant to facilitate the concealment of funds used to support terrorist activities. This section accordingly amends 18 U.S.C. §2339A to include expert services and assistance, making the offense applicable to experts who provide services or assistance knowing or intending that the services or assistance is to be used in preparing for or carrying out terrorism crimes. This section also amends 18 U.S.C. §2339A to conform its coverage of terrorism crimes to the more complete list specified in section 309 of the bill ('Federal terrorism offenses')," *DoJ* at 306.

[114]*U.S.Const.* Art.III, §2, cl.3; Amend. IV; *United States v. Cabrales*, 524 U.S. 1 (1998); *United States v. Rodriguez-Moreno*, 526 U.S. 275 (1999).

acquiring or operating, through the patterned commission of any of a series of predicate offenses, an enterprise whose activities affect interstate or foreign commerce, 18 U.S.C. 1961.[115]

Prior law, 18 U.S.C. 2325-2327, outlawed violation of Federal Trade Commission (FTC) telemarketing regulations promulgated under 15 U.S.C. 6101 *et seq*. Section 1011 of the Act brings fraudulent charitable solicitations within the FTC's regulatory authority.[116]

New Penalties

The Act increases the penalties for acts of terrorism and for crimes which terrorists might commit. More specifically it establishes an alternative maximum penalty for acts of terrorism, raises the penalties for conspiracy to commit certain terrorist offenses, envisions sentencing some terrorists to life-long parole, and increases the penalties for counterfeiting, cybercrime, and charity fraud.

The Justice Department suggested an alternative term of imprisonment up to life imprisonment for anyone convicted of an offense designated a terrorist crime. It characterized its proposal as analogous to the standard fine provisions of 18 U.S.C. 3571(b),(c). Section 3571 sets a basic maximum fine of $250,000 for any individual who convicted of a federal felony notwithstanding any lower maximum fine called for in the statute that outlaws the offense.[117]

---

[115]"The list of predicate federal offenses for RICO, appearing in 18 U.S.C. §1961(1), includes none of the offenses which are most likely to be committed by terrorists. This section adds terrorism crimes to the list of RICO predicates, so that RICO can be used more frequently in the prosecution of terrorist organizations. As in various other provisions, the list of offenses in section 309 of the bill ('Federal terrorism offenses') is used in identifying the relevant crimes," *DoJ*, at §304.

[116]For a general discussion, *see*, Wellborn, *Combating Charitable Fraud: An Overview of State and Federal Law*, CRS REP.NO. RS21058 (Nov. 7, 2001).

[117]"Under existing law, the maximum prison terms for federal offenses are normally determined by specifications in the provisions which define them. These provisions can provide inadequate maxima in cases where the offense is aggravated by its terrorist character or motivation. This section accordingly adds a new subsection (e) to 18 U.S.C. §3559 which provides alternative maximum prison terms, including imprisonment for any term of years or for life, for crimes likely to be committed by terrorists. This is analogous to the maximum fine provisions of 18 U.S.C. §3571(b)-(c) – which supersede lower fine amounts specified in the statutes defining particular offenses – and will more consistently ensure the availability of sufficiently high maximum penalties in terrorism cases. As in several other provisions of this bill, the list of the serious crimes most frequently committed by terrorists set forth in section 309 of the bill ('Federal terrorism offenses' is used in defining the scope of the provision," *DoJ*, at §302.

The proposal, however, failed to identify the critical elements that would trigger the alternative.[118] Both practical and constitutional challenges might be thought to attend this failure to distinguish between those convicted of some "garden variety" crime of terrorism and the more serious offender meriting the alternative, supplementary penalty. Perhaps for this reason, the Act opted to simply increase the maximum penalties for various crimes of terrorism, particularly those which involve the taking of a human life and are not already capital offenses, section 810. Thus, it increases the maximum terms imprisonment for:

- for life-threatening arson or arson of a dwelling committed within a federal enclave, from 20 years to any term of years or life, 18 U.S.C. 81;
- for causing more than $100,000 in damage to, or significantly impairing the operation of an energy facility, from 10 to 20 years (or any term of years or life, if death results), 18 U.S.C. 1366;
- for providing material support to a terrorist or a terrorist organization, from 10 to 15 years (or any term of years or life, if death results), 18 U.S.C. 2339A, 2339B;
- for destruction of national defense materials, from 10 to 20 years (or any term of years or life, if death results), 18 U.S.C. 2155;
- for sabotage of a nuclear facility, from 10 to 20 years (or any term of years or life, if death results), 42 U.S.C. 2284;
- for carrying a weapon or explosive abroad an aircraft with U.S. special aircraft jurisdiction, from 15 to 20 years (or any term of years or life, if death results), 49 U.S.C. 46505; and
- for sabotage of interstate gas pipeline facilities, from 15 to 20 years (or any term of years or life, if death results), 49 U.S.C. 60123.

It is a separate federal offense punishable by imprisonment for not more than five years to conspire to commit any federal felony, 18 U.S.C. 371. Co-conspirators are likewise subject to punishment for the underlying offense and for any other crimes committed in furtherance of the conspiracy. Nevertheless, some federal criminal statutes impose the same penalties for

[118] "A person convicted of any Federal terrorism offense may be sentenced to imprisonment for any term of years or for life, notwithstanding any maximum term of imprisonment specified in the law describing the offense. The authorization of imprisonment under this subsection is supplementary to, and does not limit, the availability of any other penalty authorized by the law describing the offense, including the death penalty, and does not limit the applicability

both the crimes they proscribe and any conspiracy to commit them. The Justice Department urged similar treatment for crimes of terrorism.[119] Again, the Act, in section 811, opts for a less sweeping approach and establishes equivalent sanctions for conspiracy and the underlying offense in cases of:

- arson committed within a federal enclave, 18 U.S.C. 81;
- killing committed while armed with a firearm in a federal building, 18 U.S.C. 930(c);
- destruction of communications facilities, 18 U.S.C. 1362;
- destruction of property within a federal enclave, 18 U.S.C. 1363;
- causing a train wreck, 18 U.S.C. 1922;
- providing material support to a terrorist, 18 U.S.C. 2339A;
- torture committed overseas under color of law, 18 U.S.C. 2340A;
- sabotage of a nuclear facility, 42 U.S.C. 2284;
- interfering with a flight crew within U.S. special aircraft jurisdiction, 49 U.S.C. 46504;
- carrying a weapon or explosive abroad an aircraft within U.S. special aircraft jurisdiction, 49 U.S.C. 46505; and
- sabotage of interstate gas pipeline facilities, 49 U.S.C. 60123.

When federal courts impose a sentence of a year or more upon a convicted defendant, they must also impose a term of supervised release, 18 U.S.C. 3583; U.S.S.G. §5D1.1. Supervised release is not unlike parole, except that it is ordinarily imposed in addition to (rather than in lieu of) a term, or portion of a term, of imprisonment. The term may be no longer than 5 years for most crimes and violations of the conditions of release may result in imprisonment for up to an additional 5 years, 18 U.S.C. 3583(e). The

---

of any mandatory minimum term of imprisonment, including any mandatory life term, provided by the law describing the offense," *Draft* at §302.

[119] "The maximum penalty under the general conspiracy provision of federal criminal law (18 U.S.C. §371) is five years, even if the object of the conspiracy is a serious crime carrying a far higher maximum penalty. For some individual offenses and types of offense, special provisions authorize conspiracy penalties equal to the penalties for the object offense – see e.g., 21 U.S.C. §846 (drug crimes) – but there is no consistently applicable provision of this type for the crimes that are likely to be committed by terrorists.

"This section accordingly adds a new §2332c to the terrorism chapter of the criminal code – parallel to the drug crime conspiracy provision in 21 U.S.C. §846 – which provides maximum penalties for conspiracies to commit terrorism crimes that are equal to the maximum penalties authorized for the objects of such conspiracies. This will more consistently provide adequate penalties for terrorist conspiracies. As in various other provisions of this bill, the relevant class of offenses is specified by the notion of 'Federal terrorism offense,' which is defined in section 309 of the bill," *DoJ* at §303.

terms of supervisory release for drug dealers, however, are often cast as mandatory minimums with no statutory ceiling. Thus, for example, a dealer convicted of distributing more than a kilogram of heroin must receive a term of supervised release of "at least 5 years" in addition to a term of imprisonment imposed for the offense, 21 U.S.C. 841(b). Although a majority feel that the more specific drug provisions of 21 U.S.C. 841 trump the more general limitations of 18 U.S.C. 3583, some of the federal appellate courts believe the two should be read in concert where possible (*e.g.*, at least but not more than 5 years).[120] The Justice Department recommended a maximum supervisory term of life for those convicted of acts of terrorism (subject to the calibrations of the Sentencing Commission),[121] a recommendation which the Act accepted in section 812 but only in the case of terrorists whose crimes resulted in death or were marked by a foreseeable risk of death or serious bodily injury, 18 U.S.C. 3583(j).

Sometime ago, Congress outlawed computer fraud and abuse (cybercrime) involving "federal protected computers" (*i.e.*, those owned or used by the federal government or by a financial institution or used in interstate or foreign commerce), 18 U.S.C. 1030. Section 814 of the Act increases the penalty for intentionally damaging a protected computer from imprisonment for not more than 5 years to imprisonment for not more than

[120] *Compare, United States v. Barragan*, 263 F.3d 919, 925-26 (9th Cir. 2001); *United States v. Pratt*, 239 F.3d 640, 646-48 (4th Cir. 2001); *United States v. Heckard*, 238 F.3d 1222, 1237 (10th Cir. 2001); and *United States v. Aguayo-Delgado*, 220 F.3d 926, 933 (8th Cir. 2000); *with, United States v. Meshack*, 225 F.3d 556, 578 (5th Cir. 2001); and *United States v. Samour*, 199 F.3d 821, 824-25 (6th Cir. 2001).

[121] "Existing federal law (18 U.S.C. 3583(b)) generally caps the maximum period of post-imprisonment supervision for released felons at 3 or 5 years. Thus, in relation to a released but still unreformed terrorist, there is no means of tracking the person or imposing conditions to prevent renewed involvement in terrorist activities beyond a period of a few years. The drug laws (21 U.S.C. §841) mandate longer supervision periods for persons convicted of certain drug trafficking crimes, and specify no upper limit on the duration of supervision, but there is nothing comparable for terrorism offenses.

"This section accordingly adds a new subsection to 18 U.S.C. 3583 to authorize longer supervision periods, including potentially lifetime supervision, for persons convicted of terrorism crimes. This would permit appropriate tracking and oversight following release of offenders whose involvement with terrorism may reflect lifelong ideological commitments. As in other provisions in this bill, the covered class of crimes is federal terrorism offenses, which are specified in section 390 of the bill.

"This section affects only the maximum periods of post-release supervision allowed by statute. It does not limit the authority of the Sentencing Commission and the courts to tailor the supervision periods imposed in particular cases to offense and offender characteristics, and the courts will retain their normal authority under 18 U.S.C. §3583(e)(1) to terminate supervision if it is no longer warranted," *DoJ* at §308.

10 years (from not more than 10 to not more than 20 years for repeat offenders).[122]

Finally, section 1011 increases the penalty for fraudulently impersonating a Red Cross member or agent (18 U.S.C. 917) from imprisonment for not more than 1 year to imprisonment for not more than 5 years.

Other Procedural Adjustments

In other procedural adjustments designed to facilitate criminal investigations, the Act:

- increases the rewards for information in terrorism cases
- expands the Posse Comitatus Act exceptions
- authorizes "sneak and peek" search warrants
- permits nationwide and perhaps worldwide execution of warrants in terrorism cases
- eases government access to confidential information
- allows the Attorney General to collect DNA samples from prisoners convicted of any crime of violence or terrorism
- lengthens the statute of limitations applicable to crimes of terrorism
- clarifies the application of federal criminal law on American installations and in residences of U.S. government personnel overseas
- adjusts federal victims' compensation and assistance programs

A section found in the Senate bill, but ultimately dropped, would have changed the provision of law that required Justice Department prosecutors to adhere to the ethical standards of the legal profession where they conduct their activities (the McDade-Murtha Amendment), 28 U.S.C. 530B.[123]

---

[122]It provides a comparable increase to not more than 20 years (from not more than 10 years) for those who recklessly damage a protected computer following a prior computer abuse conviction. Civil and criminal liability for simply causing protected computer damage (as opposed to intentionally or reckless causing the damage) is limited to special circumstances, *e.g.*, damage in excess of $5000, damage causing physical injury, etc.; section 814 adds to the list of circumstances upon which liability may be predicated. To the list of predicate circumstances, it adds causing damage to a computer used by the government for the administration of justice, national defense, or national security.

[123]When presenting the final bill to the House, the Chairman of the Judiciary Committee noted, "the Senate bill contained revisions of the so-called McDade law. This compromise version does not contain those changes, and I agreed to review this subject in a different context,"

Rewards

The Attorney General already enjoys the power to pay rewards in criminal cases, but his powers under other authorities is often subject to caps on the amount he might pay. Thus as a general rule, he may award amounts up to $25,000 for the capture of federal offenders, 18 U.S.C. 3059, and may pay rewards in any amount in recognition of assistance to the Department of Justice as long as the Appropriations and Judiciary Committees are notified of any rewards in excess of $100,000, 18 U.S.C. 3059B. Although he has special reward authority in terrorism cases, individual awards were capped at $500,000, the ceiling for the total amount paid in such rewards was $5 million, and rewards of $100,000 or more required his personal approval or that of the President, 18 U.S.C. 3071-3077. Over the last several years, annual appropriation acts have raised the $500,000 cap to $2 million and the $5 million ceiling to $10 million, *e.g.*, P.L. 106-553, 114 Stat. 2762-67 (2000); P.L. 106-113, 113 Stat. 1501A-19 (1999); P.L.105-277, 112 Stat. 2681-66 (1998).

The Act supplies the Attorney General with the power to pay rewards to combat terrorism in any amount and without an aggregate limitation, but for rewards of $250,000 or more it insists on personal approval of the Attorney General or the President and on notification of the Appropriations and Judiciary Committees, section 501 (18 U.S.C. 3071). In addition, the counterterrorism fund of section 101 can be used "without limitation" to pay rewards to prevent, investigate, or prosecute terrorism.[124]

The Secretary of State's reward authority was already somewhat more generous than that of the Attorney General. He may pay rewards of up to $5 million for information in international terrorism cases as long as he personally approves payments in excess $100,000, 22 U.S.C. 2708. The Act removes the $5 million cap and allows rewards to be paid for information concerning the whereabouts of terrorist leaders and facilitating the dissolution of terrorist organizations, section 502.

Posse Comitatus

The Posse Comitatus Act and its administrative auxiliaries, 18 U.S.C. 1385, 10 U.S.C. 375, ban use of the armed forces to execute civilian law, absent explicit statutory permission. One existing statutory exception covers

147 *Cong.Rec.* H7196 (daily ed. Oct. 23, 2001)(remarks of Rep. Sensenbrenner); for general background, *see*, Doyle, *McDade-Murtha Amendment: Ethical Standards for Justice Department Attorneys*, CRS REP.NO. RL30060 (Dec. 14, 2001).

[124] The fund is otherwise available to reestablish capacity lost in terrorist attacks, to conduct threat assessments for federal agencies, and to reimburse federal agencies for the costs of detaining terrorist suspects overseas.

Department of Justice requests for technical assistance in connection with emergencies involving biological, chemical or nuclear weapons, 18 U.S.C. 2332e, 10 U.S.C. 382. The Act enlarges the exception to include emergencies involving other weapons of mass destruction, section 104.[125]

Delayed Notification of a Search (Sneak and Peek)

Rule 41 of the Federal Rules of Criminal Procedure seemed to preclude "sneak and peek" warrants before passage of the Act. A sneak and peek warrant is one that authorizes officers to secretly enter, either physically or virtually; conduct a search, observe, take measurements, conduct examinations, smell, take pictures, copy documents, download or transmit computer files, and the like; and depart without taking any tangible evidence or leaving notice of their presence. The Rule required that after the execution of a federal search warrant officers leave a copy of the warrant and an inventory of what they have seized (tangible or intangible), and they were to advise the issuing court what they had done, F.R.Crim.P. 41(d). To what extent did Rule 41 portray the standards for a reasonable search and seizure for purposes of the Fourth Amendment?

The Fourth Amendment clearly requires officers to knock and announce their purpose before entering to execute a warrant, *Richards v. Wisconsin*, 520 U.S. 385 (1997), but with equal clarity recognizes exceptions for exigent circumstances such as where compliance will lead to the destruction of evidence, flight of a suspect, or endanger the officers, *Wilson v. Arkansas*, 514 U.S. 927 (1995). It is undisputed that Title III (the federal wiretap statute) is not constitutionally invalid because it permits delayed notice of the installation of an interception device, *Dalia v. United States*, 441 U.S. 238 (1979). Finally, there is no doubt that the Fourth Amendment imposes no demands where it does not apply. Thus, chapter 121 (court authorization for disclosure of the contents of e-mail stored with third party service providers) may permit delayed notification of the search of e-mail in remote storage with a third party for more than 180 days without offending the Fourth Amendment, because there is no Fourth Amendment justifiable expectation of privacy under such circumstances, *cf., United States v. Miller*, 425 U.S. 435 (1976).

The lower federal courts are divided over the extent to which the Rule reflects Fourth Amendment requirements. The Ninth Circuit saw the Fourth Amendment reflected in Rule 41, *United States v. Freitas*, 800 F.2d 1451,

---

[125]For a general discussion of the Posse Comitatus Act, *see*, Doyle, *The Posse Comitatus Act & Related Matters: The Use of the Military to Execute Civilian Law*, CRS REP.NO. 95-964 (June 1, 2000).

1453 (9th Cir.1986).[126] The Second Circuit was less convinced and preferred to hold sneak and peek searches to the demands of Rule 41, *United States v. Pangburn*, 983 F.2d 449 (2d Cir. 1993).[127] The Fourth Circuit was, if

---

[126]"The district court held that a search warrant permitting agents to observe, but not seize tangible property was impermissible under Rule 41. That holding conflicts with language in *United States v. New York Telephone Co.*, 434 U.S. 159, 169 (1977): Although Rule 41(h) defines property to include documents, books, papers, and any other tangible objects, it does not restrict or purport to exhaustively enumerate all the items which may be seized pursuant to Rule 41.... Rule 41 is not limited to tangible items. That case held seizures of intangibles were not precluded by the definition of property appearing in Rule 41(b). Without doubt there was a search in this case. Its purpose, we hold, was to seize intangible, not tangible, property. The intangible property to be seized was information regarding the status of the suspected clandestine methamphetamine laboratory. The search was authorized by a warrant supported by what the district court concluded was probable cause.... The question remains, however, whether a warrant lacking both a description of the property to be seized and a notice requirement conforms to Rule 41....we hold that there was no compliance with Rule 41 under the facts of this case.... While it is clear that the Fourth Amendment does not prohibit all surreptitious entries, it is also clear that the absence of any notice requirement in the warrant casts strong doubt on its constitutional adequacy. We resolve those doubts by holding that in this case the warrant was constitutionally defective in failing to provide explicitly for notice within a reasonable, but short, time subsequent to the surreptitious entry. Such time should not exceed seven days except upon a strong showing of necessity. We take this position because surreptitious searches and seizures of intangibles strike at the very heart of the interests protected by the Fourth Amendment. The mere thought of strangers walking through and visually examining the center of our privacy interests, our home, arouses our passion for freedom as does nothing else. That passion, the true source of the Fourth Amendment, demands that surreptitious entries be closely circumscribed," *United States v. Freitas (Freitas I)*, 800 F.2d 1451, 1455-456 (9th Cir. 1986). The court remanded the case for a determination of whether grounds existed for a good faith exception to application of the exclusionary rule. It subsequently declined to exclude the evidence on those grounds, *United States v. Freitas (Freitas II)*, 856 F.2d 1425 (9th Cir. 1988).

[127]"No provision specifically requiring notice of the execution of a search warrant is included in the Fourth Amendment. Accordingly, in *Dalia v. United States*, 441 U.S. 238, 247 (1979), the Supreme Court found no basis for a constitutional rule proscribing all covert entries. Resolving the particular issue raised in *Dalia*, the Court determined that the Fourth Amendment does not prohibit per se a covert entry performed for the purpose of installing otherwise legal electronic bugging equipment. Rule 41 of the Federal Rules of Criminal Procedure does require notice of the execution of a search warrant but does not prescribe when the notice must be given. Rule 41 by its terms provides for notice only in the case of seizures of physical property.... The Supreme Court also has held that the authority conferred by Rule 41 is not limited to the seizure of tangible items. *See United States v. New York Telephone Co.*, 434 U.S. 159, 169 (1977). Despite the absence of notice requirements in the Constitution and Rule 41, it stands to reason that notice of a surreptitious search must be given at some point after the covert entry....Although the *Freitas I* court specifically determined that the warrant was constitutionally defective for failure to include a notice requirement, we made no such determination in *United States v. Villegas*, 899 F.2d 1324 (1999). Although the *Freitas I* court found that covert entry searches without physical seizure strike at the very heart of the Fourth Amendment-protected interests, we used no such language in *Villegas*. Indeed, it was our perception that a covert entry search for intangibles is less intrusive than a conventional search with physical seizure because the latter deprives the owner not only of privacy but also of the use of his property.... We prefer to root out notice requirement in the provisions of Rule 41 rather than in the somewhat amorphous Fourth Amendment interests concept developed by the *Freitas I* court. The

anything, less convinced. Moreover, the facts in the case demonstrate the potential impact of the issue on computer privacy, *United States v. Simons*, 206 F.3d 392 (4th Cir. 2000).[128]

The Justice Department urged that the conflict be resolved with a uniform rule which permitted sneak and peek warrants under the same circumstances that excused delayed notification of government access to e-mail to longer-term, remote, third party storage.[129]

Fourth Amendment does not deal with notice of any kind, but Rule 41 does. It is from the Rule's requirements for service of a copy of the warrant and for provision of an inventory that we derive the requirements of notice in cases where a search warrant authorizes covert entry to search and to seize intangibles," *United States v. Pangburn*, 983 F.2d 449, 453-55 (2d Cir. 1993).

[128]In *Simons*, a search team entered Simons' office at night in his absence and "copied the contents of Simons' computer; computer diskettes found in Simons' desk drawer; computer files stored on the zip drive or on zip drives diskettes; videotapes; and various documents, including personal correspondence. No original evidence was removed from the office. Neither a copy of the warrant nor a receipt for the property seized was left in the office or otherwise given to Simons at that time, and Simons did not learn of the search for approximately 45 days." A property list, however, was returned to the magistrate. In the view of the Fourth Circuit, "[t]here are two categories of Rule 41 violations; those involving constitutional violations and all others. The violations termed 'ministerial' in our prior cases obviously fall into the latter category. Nonconstitutional violations of Rule 41 warrant suppression only when the defendant is prejudiced by the violation, or when there is evidence of intentional and deliberate disregard of a provision in the Rule. First, we conclude that the failure of the team executing the warrant to leave either a copy of the warrant or a receipt for the items taken did not render the search unreasonable under the Fourth Amendment. The Fourth Amendment does not mention notice, and the Supreme Court has stated that the constitution does not categorically proscribe covert entries, which necessarily involve a delay in notice. And insofar as the August search satisfied the requirements of the Fourth Amendment, *i.e.*, it was conducted pursuant to a warrant based on probable cause issued by a neutral and detached magistrate, we perceive no basis for concluding that the 45-day delay in notice rendered the search unconstitutional. Having concluded that the Rule 41(d) violation at issue here did not infringe on Simons' constitutional rights, we must now evaluate his argument that the violation was deliberate.... The district court did not address the intent issue when it ruled on Simons' motion to suppress.... We therefore remand for the district court to consider whether the Government intentionally and deliberately disregarded the notice provision of Rule 41(d) when it carried out the August 6, 1998 search," 206 F.3d at 403.

[129]"The law that currently governs notice to subjects of warrants where there is a showing to the court that immediate notice would jeopardize an ongoing investigation or otherwise interfere with lawful law enforcement activities, is a mix of inconsistent rules, practices, and court decisions varying widely from jurisdiction to jurisdiction across the country. This greatly hinders the investigation of many terrorism cases and other cases. This section resolves this problem by establishing a statutory, uniform standard for all such circumstances. It incorporates by reference the familiar, court-enforced standards currently applicable to stored communications under 18 U.S.C. §2705, and applies them to all instances where the court is satisfied that immediate notice of execution of a search warrant would jeopardize an ongoing investigation or otherwise interfere with lawful law-enforcement activities," *DoJ* at §353.

The Act, in section 213, stops short of the Justice Department proposal. Characterized as a codification of the Second Circuit decision, 147 *Cong.Rec.* H7197 (daily ed. Oct. 23, 2001), the Act extends the delayed notification procedure of chapter 121, which operates in an area to which the Fourth Amendment is inapplicable, to cases to which the Fourth Amendment applies, 18 U.S.C. 3103a. Its sneak and peek authorization reaches all federal search and seizure warrants where the court finds reasonable cause to believe that notification would have the kind of adverse results depicted in 18 U.S.C. 2705. Section 2705 describes both exigent circumstances (*e.g.*, risk of destruction of evidence or bodily injury) and circumstances that are not likely to excuse notification when it is required by the Fourth Amendment (*e.g.*, jeopardizing an investigation; delaying a trial). The sneak and peek authorization, however, does not reach tangible evidence, or wire or electronic communication unless the court finds the seizure "reasonably necessary." It is not clear whether reasonable necessity means a seizure necessary to the investigation that is also reasonable in a Fourth Amendment sense, *i.e.*, in the presence of exigent circumstances, or whether it means a seizure which a reasonable judge might find necessary for the investigation.[130] The doctrine of constitutional avoidance argues against the latter interpretation. By the same token, when the Act permits delay for a reasonable period, it should probably be understood to mean constitutionally "reasonable," that is, a brief period reasonable in light of the exigent circumstances which allow the delay or their like.

Nationwide Terrorism Search Warrants

The Fourth Amendment demands that warrants be issued by a neutral magistrate, *Coolidge v. New Hampshire*, 403 U.S. 443 (1971); the Sixth Amendment, that crimes be prosecuted in the districts where they occur, *United States v. Cabrales*, 524 U.S. 1 (1998). The Federal Rules direct magistrates to issue warrants only for property within their judicial district, although they permit execution outside the district for property located in the district when the warrant is sought but removed before execution can be had, F.R.Crim.P. 41(a).

The Act, in section 219, allows a magistrate in the district in which a crime of terrorism has occurred to issue a search warrant to be executed either "within or outside the district," (F.R.Crim.P. 41(a)(3)) in domestic and

[130]Since neither the restriction nor its reasonable necessity exception appeared in the Justice Department's initial proposal, the Department's justification does not address the question.

international terrorism cases.[131] The provision may anticipate execution both in this country and overseas.[132] The Fourth Amendment does not apply to the overseas searches of the property of foreign nationals, *United States v. Verdugo-Urquidez*, 494 U.S. 259 (1990). It does apply to the search of American property overseas involving American authorities, although the lower federal courts are divided over the exact level of participation required to trigger coverage.[133] Neither Rule 41 nor any other provision of federal law

[131]The amended rule uses the definitions of domestic and international terrorism found in 18 U.S.C. 2331, as modified by section 802 of the Act: "(1) the term 'international terrorism' means activities that – (A) involve violent acts or acts dangerous to human life that are a violation of the criminal laws of the United States or of any State, or that would be a criminal violation if committed within the jurisdiction of the United States or of any State, (B) appear to be intended – (i) to intimidate or coerce a civilian population; (ii) to influence the policy of a government by intimidation or coercion; or (iii) to affect the conduct of a government by mass destruction, assassination or kidnapping; and (C) occur primarily outside the territorial jurisdiction of the United States, or transcend national boundaries in terms of the means by which they are accomplished, the persons they appear intended to intimidate or coerce, or the locale in which their perpetrators operate or seek asylum...(5) the term 'domestic terrorism' means activities that – (A) involve acts dangerous to human life that are a violation of the criminal laws of the United States or of any State; (B) appear to be intended – (i) to intimidate or coerce a civilian population; (ii) to influence the policy of a government by intimidation or coercion; or (iii) to affect the conduct of a government by mass destruction, assassination or kidnapping; and (C) occur primarily within the territorial jurisdiction of the United States," 18 U.S.C. 2331(1),(5).

[132]The Justice Department, with whom the proposal originated, was somewhat cryptic on this point. Its analysis suggests execution in one of the several judicial districts of the United States, but not so precisely as to negate any other construction. "The restrictiveness of the existing rule creates unnecessary delays and burdens for the government in the investigation of terrorist activities and networks that span a number of districts, since warrants must be separately obtained in each district. This section resolves that problem by providing that warrants can be obtained in any district in which activities related to the terrorism may have occurred, regardless of where the warrants will be executed," *DoJ* at §351.

[133]*United States v. Barona*, 56 F.3d 1087, 1092 (9th Cir. 1995)("United States agents' participation in the investigation is so substantial that the action is a joint venture between United States and foreign officials"); *United States v. Behety*, 32 F.3d 503, 510 (11th Cir. 1994)("if American law enforcement officials substantially participated in the search or if the foreign officials conducting the search were actually acting as agents for their American counterparts"); *United States v. Maturo*, 982 F.2d 57, 61 (2d Cir. 1992)("where the conduct of foreign law enforcement officials rendered them agents, or virtual agents, of United States law enforcement officials" or "where the cooperation between the United States and foreign law enforcement agencies is designed to evade constitutional requirements applicable to American officials"); *United States v. Mitro*, 880 F.2d 1480, 1482 (1st Cir. 1989)("where American agents participated in the foreign search or the foreign officers acted as agents for their American counterparts"); *United States v. Mount*, 757 F.2d 1315, 1318 (D.C.Cir. 1985)("if American officials or officers participated in some significant way"); *United States v. Marzano*, 537 F.2d 257, 270 (7th Cir. 1976)(declining to adopt the "joint venture" standards, but finding level of American participation in the case before it insignificant); *United States v. Morrow*, 537 F.2d 120, 139 (5th Cir. 1976)("if American law enforcement officials participated in the foreign search, or if the foreign authorities actually conducting the search were acting as agents for their American counterparts"); each of the decisions also

apparently contemplated extraterritorial execution, *cf.*, F.R.Crim.P.41, *Advisory Committee Notes: 1990 Amendment* (discussing a proposal for extraterritorial execution that the Supreme Court rejected).[134]

If the Act anticipates overseas execution there may be some question whether it creates a procedure to be used in lieu of extradition when the person for whom the search warrant has been issued is located outside the United States. The section refers to warrants for "search of property *or for a person* within or outside the district," §219 (emphasis added). The Judicial Conference in 1990 recommended an amendment to Rule 41, which the Supreme Court rejected, that would have permitted the overseas execution of federal search warrants. In doing so, the Conference suggested extraterritorial execution be limited to warrants to search for property and not reach warrants to search for persons, "lest the rule be read as a substitute for extradition proceedings," F.R.Crim.P. 41, *Advisory Committee Notes: 1990 Amendment.* There is no indication, however, that the section is at odds with either the Fourth or Sixth Amendment.

Terrorists' DNA

The courts have generally concluded that the collection of DNA information from convicted prisoners does not offend constitutional standards *per se*.[135] Existing federal law allowed the Attorney General to collect samples from federal prisoners convicted of a variety of violent crimes, 42 U.S.C. 14135a. The Act enlarges the predicate offense list to include any crime of violence or any terrorism offense, section 503.[136]

---

suggests that evidence secured in a manner which shocked the conscience of the court would be excluded.

[134]The Code still carries remnants of the consular courts which speak of the overseas execution of arrest warrants in places where the United States has "extraterritorial jurisdiction," 18 U.S.C. 3042. The history of the provisions makes it clear that the phrase "extraterritorial jurisdiction" was intended to coincide with those places in which the U.S. had consular courts, *see*, S.Rep. 217, 73d Cong., 2d Sess. 3 (1934), *reprinted*, 78 *Cong.Rec.* 4982-983 (1934)("The countries to which the proposed bill, if enacted into law, would relate are the following, in which the United States exercises extraterritorial jurisdiction: China, Egypt, Ethiopia, Muscat, and Morocco"); 22 U.S.C. 141 (1926 ed.)(conferring judicial powers on consular courts there identified as those located in China, Egypt, Ethiopia, Muscat, Morocco, Siam and Turkey).

[135]*Roe v. Marcotte*, 193 F.3d 72 (2d Cir. 1999); *Shaffer v. Saffle*, 148 F.3d 1180 (10th Cir. 1998); *Rise v. Oregon*, 59 F.3d 1556 (9th Cir. 1995); *Jones v. Murray*, 962 F.2d 302 (4th Cir. 1992).

[136]Summarizing the law in place at the time, the Department of Justice argued that, "The statutory provisions governing the collection of DNA samples form convicted federal offenders (42 U.S.C. §14135a(d)) are restrictive, and do not include persons convicted for the crimes that are most likely to be committed by terrorists. DNA samples cannot now be collected even from persons federally convicted of terrorist murders in most circumstances. For example, 49 U.S.C. §46502, which applies to terrorists who murder people by hijacking

Access to Educational Records

Finally, the Act calls for an ex parte court order procedure under which senior Justice Department officials may seek authorization to collect educational records relevant to an investigation or prosecution of a crime of terrorism, section 507 (as an exception to the confidentiality requirements of the General Education Provisions Act, 20 U.S.C. 1232g), section 508 (as an exception to the confidentiality requirements of the National Education Statistics Act, 20 U.S.C. 9007).

Statute of Limitations

Prosecution for murder in violation of federal law may be initiated at any time, 18 U.S.C. 3281. A five year statute of limitations applied for most other federal crimes before passage of the Act, with a few exceptions. Among the relevant exceptions were an eight year statute of limitations for several terrorist offenses, 18 U.S.C. 3286,[137] and a ten year statute of limitations for a few arson and explosives offenses, 18 U.S.C. 3295. The Justice Department recommended the elimination of a statute of limitations in terrorism cases.[138]

---

aircraft, 18 U.S.C. §844(i), which applies to terrorists who murder people by blowing up buildings, and 18 U.S.C. 2332, which applies to terrorists who murder U.S. nationals abroad, are not included in the qualifying federal offenses for purposes of DNA sample collection under existing law. This section addresses the deficiency of the current law in relation to terrorists by extending DNA sample collection to all persons convicted of terrorism crimes," *DoJ* at §353.

For a general discussion, *see*, Fischer, *DNA Identification: Applications and Issues*, CRS REP.NO. RL30717 (Jan. 12, 2001).

[137] 18 U.S.C. 32 (destruction of aircraft or aircraft facilities), 37 (violence at international airports), 112 (assaults on foreign dignitaries), 351 (crimes of violence against Members of Congress), 1116 (killing foreign dignitaries), 1203 (hostage taking), 1361 (destruction of federal property), 1751 (crimes of violence against the President), 2280 (violence against maritime navigation), 2281 (violence on maritime platforms), 2332 (terrorist violence against Americans overseas), 2332a (use of weapons of mass destruction), 2332b (acts of terrorism transcending national boundaries), 2340A (torture); 49 U.S.C. 46502 (air piracy), 46504 (interference with a flight crew), 46505 (carrying a weapon aboard an aircraft), and 46506 (assault, theft, robbery, sexual abuse, murder, manslaughter or attempted murder or manslaughter in the special aircraft jurisdiction of the United States).

[138] "This section amends 18 U.S.C. §3286 to provide that terrorism of offenses may be prosecuted without limitation of time. This will make it possible to prosecute the perpetrators of terrorist acts whenever they are identified and apprehended.

"This section expressly provides that it is applicable to offenses committed before the date of enactment of the statute, as well as those committed thereafter. This retroactivity provision ensures that no limitation period will bar the prosecution of crimes committed in connection with the September 11, 2001 terrorist attacks. The constitutionality of such retroactive applications of changes in statutes of limitations is well-settled, See, e.g., *United States v. Grimes*, 142 F.3d 1342, 1350-51 (11th Cir. 1998); *People v. Frazer*, 982 P.2d 180 (Cal. 1999).

The Act takes less dramatic action in section 809. It eliminates the statute of limitations for any crime of terrorism[139] that risks or results in a death or serious bodily injury, 18 U.S.C. 3286. In the absence of such a risk or result, all other terrorism offenses become subject to the eight year statute of limitations unless already covered by the ten year statute for explosives and arson offenses, 18 U.S.C. 3286.

Application of the statute of limitations rarely provokes a constitutional inquiry. Nevertheless, due process precludes prosecution when it can be shown that pre-indictment delay "caused substantial prejudice to [a defendant's] rights to a fair trial and that the delay was an intentional device to gain tactical advantage over the accused."[140] Moreover, a judicial difference of opinion has appeared in those cases when an existing period of limitation is enlarged legislatively and the new period made applicable to past offenses. The lower federal courts have long noted that the Constitution

"Existing federal law (18 U.S.C. §3282) bars prosecuting most offenses after five years. 18 U.S.C. §3286, as currently formulated, extends the limitation period for prosecution for certain offenses that may be committed by terrorists – but only to eight years. While this is a limited improvement over the five-year limitation period for most federal offenses, it is patently inadequate in relation to the catastrophic human and social costs that frequently follow from such crimes as destruction of aircraft (18 U.S.C. §32), aircraft hijackings ([49] U.S.C. §§46502, 46504-06, attempted political assassinations (18 U.S.C. §§351, 1116, 1751), or hostage taking (18 U.S.C. §1203). These are not minor acts of misconduct which can properly be forgiven or forgotten merely because the perpetrator has avoided apprehension for some period of time. Anomalously, existing law provides longer limitation periods for such offenses as bank frauds and certain artwork thefts (18 U.S.C.§§3293-94) than it does for crimes characteristically committed by terrorists.

"In many American jurisdictions, the limitation periods for prosecution for serious offenses are more permissible than those found in federal law, including a number of states which have no limitation period for the prosecution of felonies generally. While this section does not go so far, it does eliminate the limitation period for prosecution of the major crimes that are most likely to be committed by terrorists ('Federal terrorism offenses'), as specified in section 309 of this bill," *DoJ* at 301.

[139] As defined by 18 U.S.C. 2332b(g)(5)(B), with the amendments of §808, this includes, in addition to the offenses already listed in 18 U.S.C. 3296 – 18 U.S.C. 81 (arson within U.S. special maritime and territorial jurisdiction); 175 & 175b (biological weapons); 229 (chemical weapons); 831 (nuclear weapons); 842(m) & (n) (plastic explosives); 844(f)(bombing federal property where death results); 844(i)(bombing property used in interstate commerce); 930(c)(possession of a firearm in a federal building where death results), 956(a)(conspiracy within the U.S. to commit murder, kidnapping, or to maim overseas); 1030(a) (1), (5)(A)(i), (5)(B)(ii)-(v)(computer abuse); 1114 (killing federal officers or employees); 1362 (destruction of communications facilities); 1363 (malicious mischief within the U.S. special maritime and territorial jurisdiction); 1366(a)(destruction of an energy facility); 1992 (train wrecking); 1993 (terrorist attack on mass transit); 2155 (destruction of national defense materials); 2339 (harboring terrorists); 2339A (material support to terrorists), 2339B (material support to terrorist organizations); 42 U.S.C. 2284 (sabotage of nuclear facilities); and 49 U.S.C. 60123(b)(destruction of pipeline facilities).

[140] *United States v. Marion*, 404 U.S. 307, 325 (1971); *United States v. Lovasco*, 431 U.S. 783, 790 (1977).

poses no impediment to enlarging a period of limitation *as long as it does not revive an expired period.*[141] Recently, however, the California Supreme Court held that retroactive revival of an expired statute of limitations offended neither the California nor the United States Constitution.[142]

Section 809 applies "to the prosecution of any offense committed before, on, or after the date of enactment of this section," the very words used in the Justice Department proposal. The Justice Department, in describing its proposal, cited both federal law (*Grimes*, where the court held that extensions may be applied where the earlier period of limitations has not expired) and California law (*Frazer*, where the court held that extensions may revive an expired period of limitations). The implication is that the Justice Department understood its proposal to apply to past offenses whether the earlier statute of limitations had expired or not. Other than its use of identical terminology, Congress gave no hint of whether it intended to adopt this view for section 809. Whether the federal courts could be persuaded to overcome their previously expressed constitutional reservations is equally uncertain.

Extraterritoriality

Crime is usually outlawed, prosecuted and punished where it is committed. In the case of the United States, this is ordinarily a matter of practical and diplomatic preference rather than constitutional necessity. Consequently, although prosecutions are somewhat uncommon, a surprising number of federal criminal laws have extraterritorial application. In some instances, the statute proscribing the misconduct expressly permits the exercise of extraterritorial jurisdiction, 18 U.S.C. 2381 (treason) ("Whoever, owing allegiance to the United States...within the United States or elsewhere..."). In others, such as those banning assassination of Members of Congress, 18 U.S.C. 351, or the murder of federal law enforcement officers, 18 U.S.C. 1114, the courts have assumed Congress intended the prohibitions to have extraterritorial reach.[143]

---

[141] *United States v. De La Matta*, 266 F.3d 1275, 1286 (11th Cir. 2001); *United States v. Grimes*, 142 F.3d 1342, 1351 (11th Cir. 1998); *United States v. Morrow*, 177 F.3d 272, 294 (5th Cir. 1999); *Falter v. United States*, 23 F.2d 420, 425-26 (2d Cir. 1928).

[142] *People v. Frazer*, 24 Cal.4th 737, 759, 982 P.2d 180, 1294, 88 Cal.Rptr.2d 312, 327 (1999).

[143] *United States v. Layton*, 855 F.2d 1388 (9th Cir. 1988)(at the time of the overseas murder of Congressman Ryan for which Layton was convicted the statute was silent as to its extraterritorial application; several years later Congress added an explicit extraterritorial provision, 18 U.S.C. 351(i)); *United States v. Benitez*, 741 F.2d 1312 (11th Cir. 1984)(18 U.S.C. 1114 has since expanded to protect all federal officers and employees, including members of the armed forces and those assisting them).

The Act touches upon extraterritoriality only to a limited extent and in somewhat unusual ways. Congress has made most common law crimes – murder, sexual abuse, kidnaping, assault, robbery, theft and the like – federal crimes when committed within the special maritime and territorial jurisdiction of the United States. The special maritime and territorial jurisdiction of the United States represents two variations of extraterritorial jurisdiction.

The special maritime jurisdiction of the United States extends to the vessels of United States registry. Historically, the territorial jurisdiction of the United States was thought to reach those areas over which Congress enjoyed state-like legislative jurisdiction. For some time, those territories were located exclusively within the confines of the United States, but over the years they came to include at least temporarily, Hawaii, the Philippines, and several other American overseas territories and possessions. Recently, the lower federal courts have become divided over the question of whether laws, enacted to apply on federal enclaves within the United States and within American territories overseas, might also apply to areas in foreign countries over which the United States has proprietary control.[144]

The Act resolves the conflict by declaring within the territory of the United States those overseas areas used by American governmental entities for their activities or residences for their personnel, at least to the extent that crimes are committed by or against an American, section 804 (18 U.S.C. 7 (9)). The section is inapplicable where it would otherwise conflict with a treaty obligation or where the offender is covered by the Military Extraterritorial Jurisdiction Act, 18 U.S.C. 3261.

Victims

Federal law has provided for crime victim compensation and assistance programs for some time. Moreover, Congress enacted September 11th Victim Compensation Fund legislation before it passed the Act. Consequently, the Act's victim provisions focus on adjustments to existing programs, primarily to those of the Victims of Crime Act of 1984, 42 U.S.C. 10601 *et seq.*, and to those maintained for the benefit of public safety officers and their survivors, 42 U.S.C. 3796 *et seq.*

[144] *Compare, United States v. Gatlin*, 216 F.3d 207 (2d Cir. 2000); *United States v. Laden*, 92 F.Supp.2d 189 (S.D.N.Y. 2000); *with, United States v. Corey*, 232 F.3d 1166 (9th Cir. 2000); *United States v. Erdos*, 474 F.2d 157 (4th Cir. 1973).

Public safety officers - police officers, firefighters, ambulance and rescue personnel - killed or disabled in the line of duty (and their heirs) are entitled to federal benefits. Prior to the Act, death benefits were set at $100,000 and the total amount available for disability benefits in a given year was capped at $5 million, 42 U.S.C. 3796 (2000 ed.). No benefits could be paid for suicides, if the officer was drunk or grossly negligent, if the beneficiary contributed to the officer's death or injury, or if the officer were employed other than in a civilian capacity, 42 U.S.C. 3796 (2000 ed.). The Act increases the death benefit to $250,000 (retroactive to January 1, 2001), section 613; and for deaths and disability connected with acts of terrorism waives the $5 million disability cap and the disqualifications for gross negligence, contributing cause, or employment in a noncivilian capacity, section 611.

Most of fines collected for violation of federal criminal laws are deposited in the Crime Victims Fund which is available for child abuse prevention and treatment grants, victim services within the federal criminal justice system, and grants to state victim compensation and victim assistance programs, 42 U.S.C. 10601 to 10608. The Act:

- authorizes private contributions to the fund (42 U.S.C. 10601(b)), section 621(a)
- instructs the Department of Justice, which administers the fund, to distribute in every fiscal year (if amounts in the Fund are sufficient) amounts equal to between 90% and 110% of the amount distributed in the previous fiscal year (120% in any year when the amount on hand is twice the amount distributed the previous year)(42 U.S.C. 10601(c)), section 621(b)
- reduces by 1% the amounts available for compensation and assistance grants (from 48.5% to 47.5% after child abuse and federal victim priorities have been met), and increases from 3% to 5% the amount available for Justice Department discretionary spending for demonstration projects and services to assist the victims of federal crimes (42 U.S.C. 10601(d), 10603(c)), section 621(c)
- converts the general reserve fund to an antiterrorism reserve fund and reduces the cap on the reserve from $100 million to $50 million (42 U.S.C. 10601(d) (5)), section 621(d)
- waives the Fund's availability caps with respect to funds transferred to it in response to the terrorist attacks of September 11 (42 U.S.C. 10601 note)), section 621(e)

- lowers the annual reduction rate on individual compensation program grants; beginning in 2003 individual grants are limited to 60% (rather than 40%) of the amount of awarded in the previous year (42 U.S.C. 10602(a)), section 622(a)
- eliminates the requirement that state compensation programs permit compensation for state residents who are the victims of terrorism overseas (42 U.S.C. 10602(b)(6)(B)), section 622(b)
- provides that compensation under the September 11th Victim Compensation Fund should be counted as income in considering eligibility for any federal indigent benefit program (42 U.S.C. 10602(c)), section 622(c)
- drops "crimes involving terrorism" from the definition of "compensable crime"; it is unclear whether the phrase was removed as redundant or pursuant to a determination to compensate victims other than through the Crime Victims Fund (42 U.S.C. 10602(d)), section 622(d)(1)
- makes it clear that the Virgin Islands is eligible to receive grants (42 U.S.C. 10602(d)), section 622(d)(2)
- adds the September 11th Victim Compensation Fund to the "double dipping" restriction that applies to the victim compensation programs and confirms that state compensation programs will not be rendered ineligible for grants by virtue of a refusal to pay dual compensation to September 11th Fund victims (42 U.S.C. 10602(e)), section 622(e)
- makes federal agencies performing law enforcement functions in the District of Columbia, Puerto Rico, the Virgin Islands, and other U.S. territories and possessions eligible for victim assistance grants (42 U.S.C. 10603(a)(6)), section 623(a)
- prohibits program discrimination against crime victims based on their disagreement with the manner in which the state is prosecuting the underlying offense (42 U.S.C. 10603(b)(1)(F)), section 623(b)
- allows Justice Department discretionary grants for purposes of program evaluation and compliance and for fellowships, clinical internships and training programs (42 U.S.C. 10603(c)(1)(A), (3)(E)), section 623(c),(e)
- reverses the preference for victim service grants over demonstration projects and training grants, so that *not more* than 50% of the amounts available for crime victim assistance grants shall be used

for victim service grants and *not less* than 50% for demonstration projects and training grants (42 U.S.C. 10603(c)(2)), section 623(d)

- makes federal and local agencies and private entities eligible for supplemental grants for services relating to victims of terrorism committed within the U.S. (42 U.S.C. 10603b(b)), section 624(a)
- allows supplemental grants for services relating to victims of terrorism committed overseas regardless of whether the victims are eligible for compensation under Title VIII of the Omnibus Diplomatic Security and Antiterrorism Act (100 Stat. 879 (1986))(Title VIII victims were previously ineligible) (42 U.S.C. 10603b(a)(1)), section 624(b)
- establishes a "double dipping" restriction under which compensation to the victims of overseas terrorism is reduced by the amount received under Title VIII of the Omnibus Act (42 U.S.C. 10603c(b)), section 624(c)

Increasing Institutional Capacity

A major portion of the Act is devoted to bolstering the institutional capacity of federal law enforcement agencies to combat terrorism and other criminal threats. In addition to the counterterrorism discussed above in the context of the Attorney General's reward prerogatives, it increases funding authorization for an FBI technical support center, section 103, and allows the FBI to hire translators without regard to otherwise applicable employment restrictions such as citizenship, section 205.

In the area of cybercrime, the Attorney General is instructed to establish regional forensic laboratories, section 817, and the Secret Service, to establish a national network of electronic crime task forces, modeled after its New York Electronic Crimes Task Force, section 105. The Act likewise clarifies the Secret Service's investigative jurisdiction with respect to computer crime (18 U.S.C. 1030) and to crimes involving credit cards, PIN numbers, computer passwords, or any frauds against financial institutions (18 U.S.C. 3056), section 506.

For a period of up to 180 days after the end of Operation Enduring Freedom, section 1010 allows the Department of Defense (DoD) to contract with state and local law enforcement authorities to perform various security functions on its military installations and facilities, 10 U.S.C. 2465.

The Act also authorizes appropriations for wide range anti-terrorism purposes including:

- $25 million a year for FY 2003 through FY 2007 for state and local terrorism prevention and antiterrorism training grants for first responders, section 1005 (28 U.S.C. 509 note)
- necessary sums (FY 2002 through FY 2007) for Office of Justice Programs (OJP) grants to state and local governments to enhance their capacity to respond to terrorist attacks, section 1014 (42 U.S.C. 3711)
- $250 million a year (FY 2002 through FY 2007) for OJP grants to state and local governments integrated information and identification systems, section 1015 (42 U.S.C. 14601)
- $50 million per fiscal year for the Attorney General to develop and support regional computer forensic laboratories (28 U.S.C. 509 note), section 816
- $50 million (FY 2002) and $100 million (FY 2003) for Bureau of Justice Assistance grants (42 U.S.C. 3796h) for federal-state-local law enforcement information sharing systems, section 701
- $20 million (FY 2002) for the activities of National Infrastructure Simulation and Analysis Center in DoD's Defense Threat Reduction Agency, section 1016 (42 U.S.C. 5195c)
- $5 million for DEA police training in South and Central Asia, section 1007.

Miscellaneous

Finally, the Act addresses the issuance of licenses for the drivers of vehicles carrying hazardous materials and the use of trade sanctions against countries that support terrorism.

The Act requires background checks for criminal records and immigration status of applicants for licenses to operate vehicles carrying hazardous materials including chemical and biological materials (49 U.S.C. 5101a), section 1012.

The Trade Sanctions Reform and Export Enhancement Act, 22 U.S.C. 7201 to 7209, limits the President's authority to unilaterally impose export restrictions on food and medical supplies. The limitations do not apply to restrictions on products that might be used for the development or production of chemical or biological weapons or of weapons of mass destruction, 22 U.S.C. 7203(2)(c). The Act expands the exception to include products that might to used for the *design* of chemical or biological weapons or of weapons of mass destruction as well, section 221(a)(1).

Only one year licenses may be issued for trade with countries that sponsor terrorism, 22 U.S.C. 7205. The Act brings areas of Afghanistan controlled by the Taliban within the same restriction, section 221(a)(2).

Neither of these changes or anything else in the trade sanctions legislation precludes the assessment of civil or criminal liability for violations of 18 U.S.C. 2339A (providing support to terrorists), of 18 U.S.C. 2339B (providing support to terrorist organizations), or of various presidential orders under the International Emergency Economic Powers Act,[145] or of restrictions on foreign involvement in weapons of mass destruction or missile proliferation, sections 221(b), 807.[146]

---

[145]*I.e.*, Executive Order No. 12947, 50 U.S.C. 1701 note (prohibiting transactions with terrorists); Executive Order No. 13224, 50 U.S.C. 1701 note (blocking property of persons who support terrorism); Executive Order No. 12978, 50 U.S.C. 1701 note (blocking assets of significant narcotics traffickers).

[146]For a general discussion of trade sanctions legislation, *see*, Jurenas, *Exempting Food and Agriculture Products from U.S. Economic Sanctions: Status and Implementation*, CRSISSUE BRIEF IB 100061.

Chapter 2

THE INTERNET AND THE USA PATRIOT ACT: POTENTIAL IMPLICATIONS FOR ELECTRONIC PRIVACY, SECURITY, COMMERCE, AND GOVERNMENT

Marcia S. Smith, Jeffrey W. Seifert, Glenn J. McLoughlin, and John Dimitri Moteff

SUMMARY

The September 11, 2001 terrorist attacks prompted congressional action on many fronts, including passage of the United and Strengthening America by Providing Appropriate Tools Required to Intercept and Obstruct Terrorism (USA PATRIOT) Act, P.L. 107-56. The Act is broadly scoped, and some of its provisions may affect Internet usage, computer security, and critical infrastructure protection.

In the area of computer security, the Act creates a definition of "computer trespasser" and makes such activities a terrorist act in certain circumstances. The Act enables law enforcement officials to intercept the communications of computer trespassers and improves their ability to track computer trespasser activities. It also codifies some elements of U.S. critical infrastructure policy articulated by both the Clinton and George W. Bush

Administrations to ensure that any disruptions to the nation's critical infrastructures are minimally detrimental.

Although the Act does not explicitly address electronic commerce (e-commerce), many of the law's provisions may impact it. In particular, Title III responds to concerns that more can be done to prevent, detect, and prosecute international money laundering and the financing of terrorism. Over time, these provisions may affect e-commerce broadly, and electronic fund transfers specifically.

Electronic government (e-government) could be affected by the Act in both positive and negative ways. The intense focus on improving data collection and information sharing practices and systems may contribute to the establishment of government-wide technical standards and best practices that could facilitate the implementation of new and existing e-government initiatives. It could also promote the utilization of secure Web portals to help ensure the data integrity of transactions between the government and citizens and business. However, concern about potential abuses of data collection provisions could dampen citizen enthusiasm for carrying out electronic transactions with the government.

The Act provides law enforcement officials with greater authority to monitor Internet activity such as electronic mail (e-mail) and Web site visits. While law enforcement officials laud their new authorities as enabling them to better track terrorist and other criminal activity, privacy rights advocates worry that, in an attempt to track down and punish the terrorists who threaten American democracy, one of the fundamental tenets of that democracy—privacy—may itself be threatened.

Because of the controversial aspects of some provisions in the Act, particularly regarding privacy, Congress and other groups are expected to monitor closely how the Act is implemented.

INTRODUCTION

The September 11, 2001 terrorist attacks prompted congressional action on many fronts, including passage of the United and Strengthening America by Providing Appropriate Tools Required to Intercept and Obstruct Terrorism (USA PATRIOT) Act. The Act is broadly scoped,[1] and some of

[1]For a detailed legal discussion of all of the provisions of the Act, see CRS Report RL31200, *Terrorism: Section by Section Analysis of the USA PATRIOT Act*, by Charles Doyle, December 10, 2001.

its provisions may affect use of the Internet, computer security, and critical infrastructure protection.

The legislation initially passed the Senate (96-1) as S. 1510 on October 11, 2001. The House passed H.R. 2975 (337-79) on October 12. A compromise bill, H.R. 3162, passed the House (under suspension) on October 24 and the Senate (98-1) on October 25. The President signed it into law on October 26 (P.L. 107-56).

The implementation of the Act will be carefully scrutinized. While law enforcement officials heralded the passage of what they regard as necessary provisions for counteracting terrorists and other criminals, civil liberties groups urged caution in passing a new law in an emotionally charged environment. During debate, some Representatives raised concerns about the process used to bring the bills to the floor. In the House, for example, the version of H.R. 2975 as reported from the Judiciary Committee on October 11 (H. Rept. 107-236, Part 1) was replaced by the text of a new bill, H.R. 3801, for the purposes of debate.[2] H.R. 3801 was very similar, but not identical, to S. 1510 as it had passed the Senate hours earlier. Hence, some Representatives felt they had insufficient time to review the legislation they were being asked to vote on. Among the changes in H.R. 3801 was an extension of the sunset period on several of the electronic surveillance provisions from 2 years to 5 years. Some Members had argued for a short sunset period, maintaining that the changes in the law were being made hurriedly. In light of this history, it appears that oversight of the Act's implementation will be of considerable interest to Congress and a broad range of interest groups.

This report summarizes the potential effect of the Act on electronic privacy, security, commerce, and government, and identifies issues that are arising.

COMPUTER SECURITY AND CRITICAL INFRASTRUCTURE PROTECTION[3]

Every day, persons gain access (or try to gain access) to other people's computers without authorization to read, copy, modify, or destroy the information contained within—webpages are defaced, unwanted messages

[2]H.R. 3801 was adopted as an amendment in the nature of a substitute to H.R. 2975.

[3]Written by John Dimitri Moteff, Specialist in Science and Technology Policy, CRS Resources, Science, and Industry Division.

and pictures are conveyed, information (or money) is stolen, communications are jammed and services denied. The list of perpetrators includes juveniles, disgruntled (ex)employees, criminals, competitors, politically or socially motivated groups, and agents of foreign governments. For the purposes of this report, people who engage in such activities will be called computer trespassers (adopting a term which the USA PATRIOT Act defines, as explained below). The damage computer trespassers can inflict, either knowingly or unwittingly, often goes beyond merely being a nuisance and in most cases rises to the level of a federal crime (pursuant to 18 U.S.C. 1030). It is also conceivable that under certain conditions such actions could be considered a terrorist act or rise to the level of endangering national security by threatening the functioning of the country's critical infrastructure.

For the most part, law enforcement agencies seem to have had adequate tools to investigate, prosecute and penalize these offenses. One area where officials have sought improvement for some time, however, is in streamlining their ability to track computer trespassers, both in real time or after the fact. Prior to passage of the USA PATRIOT Act, procedures required investigators to request court orders, warrants, subpoenas, etc. from a multitude of jurisdictions, since most computer trespassers will route their communications around the world. While the USA PATRIOT Act is directed primarily to improve the ability of the government to detect, prevent, and respond to the kinds of terrorist attacks experienced last September and October, a number of the provisions affect the government's law enforcement surveillance and investigatory powers more generally. Those that directly and indirectly affect the ability of the government to investigate, prosecute, and perhaps deter computer trespassers, whatever their intent, are listed below.

Provisions of the USA PATRIOT Act Affecting Computer Security

- Section 105 expands upon the U.S. Secret Service's National Electronic Crime Task Force Initiative. The U.S. Secret Service has been leading a New York Electronic Crime Task Force that has been held up as a model of success for investigating a variety of electronic crimes, ranging from "cloning" cell phones to denial-of-service attacks against on-line trading companies.[4] The task force includes experts from other government agencies as well as the private sector. Section 105 directs the Director of the Secret Service to develop a national network of such task forces.

- Section 202 and Section 217 clarify that law enforcement officials may seek permission to intercept electronic communications of "computer trespassers." Section 202 adds 18 U.S.C. 1030 (computer fraud and abuse) offenses to the list of offenses for which the Attorney General, or other designated officials, may authorize a request for a court order to intercept targeted communications. Section 217 defines a "computer trespasser" as someone "who accesses a protected computer[5] without authorization and thus has no reasonable expectation of privacy in any communication to, through, or from the protected computer." Section 217 also specifies the conditions under which the communications of a computer trespasser may be intercepted. Those conditions are: the owner or operator of the protected computer authorizes the interception; the person acting under color of law is lawfully engaged in an investigation; the person acting under color of law has reasonable grounds to expect the content of the computer trespasser's communication is relevant to the investigation; and the interception acquires only the trespasser's communications within the invaded computer.[6] Prior to the Act, the statute was less explicit in specifying the terms under which a computer trespasser's communications could be intercepted.
- Section 210 expands the information that law enforcement officials may obtain (with appropriate authorization) from providers of electronic communications service or remote computing services regarding a subscriber or customer of those services. The information may now include a subscriber's or customer's means and source of payment. The language is also modified to include information more clearly related to Internet use (e.g. session times

[4]See: The Cyber-Mod Squad Set Out After Crackers. Computerworld, June 19, 2000, pp. 44-45.

[5]A protected computer is defined in 18 U.S.C. 1030 (as amended by the USA PATRIOT Act) as a computer exclusively for the use of a financial institution or the U.S. government, or used by or for either of those, if the offense affects that use; any computer used in interstate or international commerce or communications; or a computer located outside the United States that is used in a manner that affects interstate or foreign commerce or communication of the United States.

[6]Earlier versions of the bill would have allowed the trespasser's communications to be intercepted wherever they were directed. The Act's more restricted language was a compromise position.

and temporarily assigned network addresses). These changes are to improve the ability of law enforcement officials to track the activity and identity of suspects concerning a wide range of offenses, including terrorist activities and those of computer trespassers.

- Section 211 clarifies that in the deregulated telecommunications environment, cable providers that also provide communication services are governed by the same statutes as other electronic communication providers in regard to interception of communications, disclosure of customer records, and application of pen registers and trap and trace devices.[7] Prior to deregulation, cable providers followed different rules. Therefore, law enforcement officials now have the same surveillance and investigatory powers in regard to cases involving cable internet services. Information regarding a subscriber's selection of video programming, however, continues to be governed separately.
- Section 216 modifies the authorities relating to use of pen registers and trap and trace devices. As a result of Section 216, a single court order authorizing the use of a pen register or trap and trace device can be used to apply those devices to any computer or facility anywhere in the country. Prior to the Act, authorization had to be obtained in each jurisdiction where the devices needed to be applied. Also, the availability of this authority with respect to computer communications was unclear. It was generally thought that these devices could only be used on telephone equipment.
- Section 220 allows a single court with jurisdiction over the offense under investigation to issue a warrant allowing the search of electronic evidence anywhere in the country. Prior to this, the warrant needed to be issued by a court within the jurisdiction where the information resided.
- Section 808 adds certain computer fraud and abuse offenses to the list of violations that may constitute a federal crime of terrorism. The new provisions apply to: anyone who knowingly accesses a computer without authorization and obtains classified information; and, anyone who knowingly causes the transmission of a program,

---

[7] A pen register allows the user to code or decode the dialing, routing, addressing, or signaling information transmitted by an instrument or facility. In terms of computer security, it allows the law enforcement official to identify the address to which a computer trespasser is sending a message. A trap and trace device allows the user to identify the source of a wire or electronic communication. In terms of computer security, it allows the law enforcement official to identify the address from which the computer trespasser is sending a message.

information, code, or command, and as a result intentionally causes damage to a protected computer. The inclusion of these offenses in the definition of a federal crime of terrorism in Section 2332b(g)(5)(B) relates primarily to who has investigatory authority over the offenses (the Attorney General, in this case). However, by virtue of cross-references in other parts of the Act, including these offenses in the definition of terrorism also affects: the extension of their statute of limitations (Section 809 of the Act); post-release supervision of someone convicted of these offenses under certain circumstances (Section 812 of the Act); and, applicability of the racketeering statutes (Section 813 of the Act). According to Section 809, should these computer offenses result in or create a foreseeable risk of death or serious bodily injury, there is no statute of limitations. Under similar conditions, Section 812 could lead to life-time post-release supervision. The cross-reference to racketeering statutes gives law enforcement officials more tools with which to prosecute computer trespassers.

- Section 814 increases the penalties for certain computer fraud and abuse offenses. The penalty for a first offense of causing the transmission of a program, information, code or command that intentionally causes damage to a protected computer increases from 5 years to 10 years. The penalty for a second such offense or a second offense of intentionally gaining unauthorized access to a protected computer and, as a result, recklessly causing damage is increased from 10 years to 20 years. Also, it is now an offense to attempt to commit these offenses. This section also redefines "damage." Damage is now defined as: i) loss to one or more persons during any 1-year period aggregating at least $5,000 in value; ii) modification or impairment, or potential modification or impairment, of the medical examination, diagnosis, treatment, or care of one or more individuals; iii) physical injury to any person; iv) a threat to public health or safety; v) damage affecting a computer system used by or for a government entity in furtherance of the administration of justice, national defense, or national security. Item "v" is new. Also, item "i" is rewritten. Prior to this, it was not clear whether the $5,000 threshold was per person affected or the total value of damages caused to all people affected. The new language clarifies that it is the latter. Finally, the Section also modifies the language in 18 U.S.C. 1030 regarding civil suits. This includes new language that says victims suffering damages resulting from an offense listed in section 1030 may not sue under this section for negligent design or manufacture of hardware, software, or firmware. This is a broad immunity that protects manufacturers should any design or manufacture problem lead to damages, including, one would expect, security vulnerabilities which are a common problem in trying to make information systems more secure.

- Section 816 authorizes the expenditure of $50 million to develop and support regional cybersecurity forensic capabilities. There are already a number of computer forensic laboratories established. This would encourage the establishment of additional ones. In addition to assisting federal authorities to investigate and prosecute computer crimes, the laboratories are to train federal, state and local officials in computer forensics, to assist state and local officials in investigating and prosecuting state and local computer offenses, and to share expertise and information on the latest developments in computer forensics.

Provisions Affecting Critical Infrastructure Protection

Since information networks (including the Internet) are considered critical infrastructures, the above sections are also relevant to this discussion. However, there are two additional provisions that affect the protection of other critical infrastructures more generally.

- Title VII is entitled Increased Information Sharing for Critical Infrastructure Protection. However, the lone section in the Title (Section 701) really addresses a set of illegal activities much broader than attacks on critical infrastructures. There exists, within the Department of Justice, a Bureau of Justice grant program that helps establish information sharing systems between federal, state, local and non-profit entities for the purpose of identifying, targeting, and removing criminal conspiracies that cross jurisdictional boundaries. These information sharing systems are to include a number of capabilities, such as rapid information retrieval and systematized updates. Section 701 would add that the information sharing system be secure. The Section also adds multi-jurisdictional terrorist conspiracies to the list of activities tracked by the information sharing system.

- Section 1016 puts into statute elements of the critical infrastructure policy that have been articulated by both the Clinton and the Bush Administrations.[8] That is, to ensure that any physical or virtual (i.e. computer-induced) disruption of the nation's critical infrastructures be rare, brief, geographically limited, manageable, and minimally detrimental to the economy, human and government services, and national security of the United States. The section defines critical infrastructure as "systems and assets, whether physical or virtual, so vital to the United States that the incapacity or destruction of such systems and assets would have debilitating impact on security, national economic security, national public health or safety, or any combination of those matters." The Section also establishes a National Infrastructure Simulation and Analysis Center. The Center is to support related counter-terrorism, threat assessment, and risk mitigation activities. In particular the Center is to model and analyze the large-scale complexity of critical infrastructures, and use those models and analyses to train authorities in incident response, to recommend changes in system designs or protections, and to provide recommendations to policymakers. The Center is to receive data from state and local governments and the private sector to assist in developing its models. The Section also authorizes the appropriation of $20 million through the Department of Defense's Defense Threat Reduction Agency to support activities at the Center.

Policy Issues

Many of the provisions related to the surveillance and investigatory powers of law enforcement have raised concerns within the privacy and civil liberties communities. These are discussed in more detail later in this report. Some of the provisions do not necessarily grant law enforcement officials more power in practice, but clarify that those powers exist and put them on a sounder basis. Many observers believe that the most important changes affecting law enforcement officials are those provisions allowing for nationwide warrants, court orders, etc. to facilitate the tracking of computer

---

[8](1) The Clinton Administration's Policy on Critical Infrastructure Protection: Presidential Decision Directive 63, White Paper, May 22, 1998. (2) President George W. Bush, Executive Order 13231—Critical Infrastructure Protection in the Information Age. Federal Register. Vol. 66. No. 202. October 18, 2001.

trespassers. In the case of investigating offenses after the fact, these provisions may save more resources than time. However, in cases where officials are trying to track computer trespassers in real time, time is of great importance and the provisions should be that much more effective. In regard to increasing the penalties for computer trespassers, there is some debate about whether doing so will have the hoped for deterrent effect.[9] Others suggest that, deterrence aside, increasing penalties better reflects the seriousness of the offenses.[10] The Act primarily strengthens law enforcement's tools to police what many believe is a network ill-designed for security. Aside from the provision to develop a National Infrastructure and Analysis Center, none of the provisions relate to providing for or ensuring more secure systems.

ELECTRONIC COMMERCE[11]

The convergence of computer and telecommunications technologies has revolutionized how we get, store, retrieve, and share information. Commercial transactions on the Internet, whether retail business-to-customer or business-to-business, are commonly called electronic commerce, or "e-commerce." Since the mid-1990s, commercial transactions on the Internet have grown substantially.[12] A January 2002 study by the Pew Internet and American Life Project found that overall, 29 million American shoppers made purchases on-line during the fourth quarter of 2001, spending an average of $392, up from $330 in the fourth quarter of 2000. A quarter of all Internet users did some shopping on the Internet last year, up from one-fifth of Internet users in 2000.

---

[9]See: Attorneys Debate Making Cybercrime Laws Tougher. Computerworld, November 20, 2000, p. 16.

[10]Ibid.

[11]Written by Glenn J. McLoughlin, Specialist in Technology and Telecommunications Policy, CRS Resources, Science, and Industry Division.

[12] For statistics and other data on e-commerce, see: CRS Report RL30435, *Internet and E-Commerce Statistics: What They Mean and Where to Find Them On the Web*, by Rita Tehan. Other sources include: [http://www.idc.com], [http://www.abcnews.go.com], [http://www.forrester.com], [http://www.emarketer.com], and [http://www.cs.cmu.edu]. It is important to note that some measurements of e-commerce, particularly data reported in the media, have not been verified.

Provisions of the USA PATRIOT Act Affecting Electronic Commerce

The USA PATRIOT Act does not address e-commerce directly;[13] however Title III of the Act, International Money Laundering Abatement and Financial Anti-Terrorism Act of 2001, addresses concerns of policymakers that, in the wake of the September 11 terrorist attacks, more can be done to prevent, detect, and prosecute international money laundering and the financing of terrorism. Title III contains three subtitles with provisions that address international money laundering, voluntary disclosure by U.S. banks of suspicious financial activity, and the bulk smuggling of currency across U.S. borders and counterfeiting.

- Subtitle A, International Counter Money Laundering and Related Measures, has among its many provisions requirements that U.S. financial institutions do more to prevent and detect money laundering actions. It requires that financial institutions provide greater monitoring and due diligence concerning certain foreign financial activities, including wire transfers, interbank accounts, and correspondent accounts involving foreign financial institutions.
- Subtitle B, Bank Secrecy Act Amendments and Related Improvements, amends previous law by revising immunity and liability provisions for financial institutions which might disclose suspicious activities and persons to the federal government, including those which may constitute an "underground" system of financial transactions.
- Subtitle C, Currency Crimes and Protection, provides new penalties for bulk cash smuggling in and out of the United States as well as counterfeiting activities.

Many of the provisions in Title III do not go into effect until regulations are promulgated.[14]

[13]It is important to note that while no provisions of the USA PATRIOT Act of 2001 explicitly address e-commerce, many provisions throughout the law may have an impact on e-commerce. See: CRS Report RL31200, op. cit., for a discussion of the complete law.

[14]See: CRS Report RL31208, International Money Laundering Abatement and Anti-Terrorist Financing Act of 2001, Title III of P.L. 107-56, by M. Maureen Murphy.

Policy Issues

Upon signing the USA PATRIOT Act, President Bush said "this legislation gives law enforcement officials better tools to put an end to financial counterfeiting, smuggling and money laundering." The President added: "We're making it easier to seize the assets of groups and individuals involved in terrorism."[15] Among the many provisions in Title III, law enforcement officials point to two of the Act's objectives—establishing new standards and requirements for increased cooperation by financial institutions when responding to federal government requests for information; and extending the federal jurisdiction over non-U.S. financial institutions in money laundering—as particularly vital to U.S. counter-terrorism efforts.[16]

However, some have raised concerns that Title III (as well as other provisions) may have a broader scope than many of its supporters intend.[17] While many are concerned that the civil liberties of individuals may be compromised if law enforcement officials extend their reach, Title III may also have implications for a wide range of e-commerce activities. It is unlikely that the Act will immediately affect retail e-commerce (e.g., online catalogue orders) or business-to-business e-commerce (e.g., the use of the Internet for inventory ordering and management). While these forms of e-commerce are growing very rapidly, to date they have not been identified as being particularly susceptible to misuse by terrorists. Retail e-commerce and business-to-business e-commerce require verifiable information between parties that may include names, addresses, credit card numbers and other information, and can be traced relatively easily. However, some observers have not ruled out terrorists using existing e-commerce exchanges to facilitate their activities in the future.[18]

The more common method of using e-commerce for illicit and terrorist purposes is through financial transactions. For example, the terrorists

---

[15] President Signs Anti-Terrorism Bill. Office of the Press Secretary. The White House. October 26, 2001.

[16] (1) Attorney General Ashcroft Directs Law Enforcement Officials to Implement New Anti-Terrorism Act. Office of Public Affairs. U.S. Department of Justice. Washington, D.C. October 26, 2001. (2) Support for Anti-Terrorism Act of 2001 (Letter to Attorney General John Ashcroft). International Association of Chiefs of Police. Alexandria, VA. October 2, 2001.

[17] Philon, Roger. First Thoughts on the New Money Laundering Act. Current Issues. The Cato Institute. Washington, D.C. December 6, 2001. [http://www.cato.org]

[18] For two views on how extensive the reach of the USA PATRIOT Act may be, see: (1) Philon, Roger. Two Kinds of Rights Current Issues. The Cato Institute, Washington, D.C. December 6, 2001 [http://www.cato.org]. (2) Chidi, George, Jr. 'Patriot Act' Aids Law Enforcement. Network World, November 5, 2001. [http://www.nwfusion.com/news/2001/1105carrier.html].

involved in the September 11 attacks reportedly used wire transfers routinely to fund their activities in the United States. Most money transfers, even relatively small amounts transferred as money orders by firms like Western Union, Money Gram, and other smaller companies, are done electronically. There is no need to establish a bank account or fill out credit reporting forms, identification requirements are minimal, a money wire firm's outlet may be located in a supermarket or drugstore and staffed by store employees, and it can take less than fifteen minutes to send money around the world.[19] The USA PATRIOT Act addresses wire transfers and money orders by requiring, among other provisions, the registration of all money order agents by December 31, 2001, and increasing the criminal penalties for those who knowingly conduct or assist in transferring money that is intended to promote or support an illegal activity. These provisions not only cover the physical transfer of money for these purposes, but electronic transfers as well.[20]

Larger financial institutions which conduct much of their business electronically—and therefore are part of the e-commerce business sector—are also affected by the USA PATRIOT Act. Among the provisions affecting large multinational financial corporations are increased authority for U.S. law enforcement officials to gain access to institutions' records and data bases; due diligence by U.S. financial institutions concerning money laundering by non-U.S. persons; enhanced standards for correspondent accounts held by U.S. banks; and prohibition of correspondent accounts with shell banks (banks which have no physical presence in their chartering country).[21]

Critics contend that the USA PATRIOT Act will not prevent nor prohibit the types of activities that terrorists engaged in before September 11. While U.S. money order and wire transfer firms will have greater reporting responsibilities and tighter restrictions under the Act, the sheer volume of transactions, many under $3,000, is enormous—in 2000, Western Union alone did 89 million wire transfers of money. Particularly in the Middle East a significant amount of money is transferred or exchanged by *hawla*, a remittance system outside of, and running parallel to, the banking system. Whether the USA PATRIOT Act can be effectively applied to terrorists' use of *hawla* is not clear. Some also question whether the time and cost to track

[19]Timmons, Heather. Terrorist Money By Wire. Business Week, November 5, 2001, p. 94.
[20]Subtitle A.
[21]CRS Report 31208, op cit, p. 4.

large portions of electronic commerce conducted through *hawla* will prove to be an efficient use of government and private sector resources.[22]

Others contend that large U.S. financial institutions may also expend significant time and resources to comply with the Act without providing any assistance in the war against terrorism. According to Ellen Zimiles, a partner in KPMG's forensics practice, a large U.S. bank spends $10 million per year to fight money laundering—and the Act may add to that cost, as well as adding new costs for brokers, insurers, and others connected with the financial industry.[23] According to another expert, a U.S. bank typically has one million to five million ATM transactions daily, and 100,000 wire transactions per day. U.S. financial institutions will likely have to address how they will balance increased security provisions, broader access to their accounts by law enforcement officials, and ensuring customers that the privacy and integrity of financial accounts will not be compromised by compliance with the Act.[24]

Abroad, many U.S. financial institutions and multinational organizations routinely transfer currency internally and externally, often crossing national borders. These institutions and corporations often engage in routine short-term lending or borrowing to balance accounts or to finance projects. There are several established mechanisms and procedures for these transactions. The London Interbank Offering Rate (LIBOR) is an overnight lending rate by which multinational corporations electronically borrow or lend money to balance their accounts. The LIBOR is set by the largest banks, and the transactions are usually made with "Eurodollars."[25] These transactions occur on a daily basis and range in the trillions of dollars. There is no indication that any U.S. institutions using the LIBOR to settle accounts have aided or abetted terrorist activities. Still, these transactions could fall under the USA PATRIOT Act. If U.S. law enforcement officials begin to examine accounts, or even seize funds, under the Act, how might multinational corporations

---

[22]Timmons, Heather. Western Union: Where the Money Is—In Small Bills. Business Week, November 26, 2001, p. 40.

[23]McNamee, Mike, et al. A Hard Slog for Financial 'Special Forces.' Business Week, November 26, 2001, p. 39-41.

[24]Ibid.

[25]"Eurodollars" are not the same as the new European currency, the Euro. Eurodollars are those dollars which are outside of the United States and used in business transactions, usually in denominations of $100,000 to $1,000,000. The term comes from the 1940s, when large amounts of U.S. dollars were pumped into European economies as part of the Marshall Plan. These dollars were so attractive as a medium for conducting business that they became a part of the European, then global, process of conducting business. See: Ritter, Lawrence S., William L. Silber, and George F. Udell. *Principles of Money, Banking and Financial Markets. (Ninth edition)*. Reading, MA, Addison-Wesley, 1997, pp. 116-117; 137-138; 220-221; 573.

react– may they even attempt to avoid compliance to the Act? Will foreign banks and governments acquiesce to U.S. actions?

Still, it is important to note that, to date, most (if not all) of the concerns raised by critics, other than those of costs of compliance, have been hypothetical. There have been no reported widespread law enforcement intrusions into financial institutions' databases, nor have there been any reported e-commerce or electronic fund transfers disruptions linked to the war on terror since the Act was signed into law. The events of September 11 resulted in a fundamental change in the way the United States views its defense and security. Over time, Title III of the USA PATRIOT Act may affect e-commerce broadly, and electronic transfers specifically. How this Act will affect law enforcement and security efforts in the Internet Age and its actual impact on privacy rights and data integrity remains to be seen.

ELECTRONIC GOVERNMENT[26]

A significant component of many of the initiatives regarding the USA PATRIOT Act specifically, and homeland security generally, involves the use of information technology to enhance existing government processes or create new ones. Some of these initiatives may contribute to the growing effort to implement e-government projects by both Congress and the Bush Administration through enhanced data sharing and greater confidence in the security and reliability of the networks. Other initiatives may inadvertently create obstacles by restricting access to information flows and reducing privacy protections.

Provisions of the USA PATRIOT Act Affecting Electronic Government

There are a number of provisions in the USA PATRIOT Act that are relevant to e-government interests. E-government involves using information technology, and especially the Internet, to improve the delivery of government services to citizens, business, and other government agencies.[27]

[26]Written by Jeffrey W. Seifert, Analyst in Information Science and Technology Policy, CRS Resources, Science, and Industry Division.

[27]For a broader discussion of e-government concepts and issues, see CRS Report RL31057, *A Primer on E-Government: Sectors, Stages, Opportunities, and Challenges of Online Governance*, Jeffrey W. Seifert; CRS Report RL30745, *Electronic Government: A*

Most of these provisions are independent of one another, reflecting the often disparate and disconnected nature of e-government initiatives. Many of the provisions in the USA PATRIOT Act related to e-government focus on government-to-government (G2G) relationships, both within the federal government, and between federal, state, local, and foreign governments. Fewer of the provisions focus on government-to-business (G2B) or government-to-customer (G2C) interactions. The relevant provisions can be found in titles III, IV, VII, IX, and X, and are briefly discussed in turn.

- Section 361 supercedes Treasury Order Number 105-08, establishes the Financial Crimes Enforcement Network (FinCEN) in statute, and charges the bureau with, among other things, establishing a financial crimes communication center to facilitate the sharing of information with law enforcement authorities. This section also requires FinCEN to maintain a government-wide data access service for information collected under anti-money laundering reporting laws, information regarding national and international currency flows, as well as information from federal, state, local, and foreign agencies and other public and private sources.
- Section 362 seeks to enhance cooperation between the federal government and the banking industry by directing the Security of Treasury to establish a "highly secure network" in FinCEN to enable financial institutions to file reports required by the Bank Secrecy Act and receive alerts regarding suspicious activities electronically.
- Section 403 emphasizes interagency data sharing and technology standards development. It authorizes appropriations to enable the State Department and the Immigration and Naturalization Service (INS) to access the Federal Bureau of Investigation's (FBI) National Crime Information Center's Interstate Identification Index (NCIC-III) database. It also directs the National Institute of Standards and Technology (NIST) to "develop and certify a technology standard that can be used to verify the identity of persons applying for a United States visa or such persons seeking to enter the United States pursuant to a visa for the purpose of conducting background checks, confirming identity, and ensuring

---

Conceptual Overview, by Harold C. Relyea; and CRS Report RL31088, *Electronic Government: Major Proposals and Initiatives*, by Harold C. Relyea.

that a person has not received a visa under a different name or such person seeking to enter the United States pursuant to a visa."

- Section 405 directs the Attorney General to carry out a study on enhancing the FBI's Integrated Automated Fingerprint Identification System (IAFIS) to improve screening of foreign nationals applying to enter the country.
- Section 413 authorizes the State Department to share, with other countries, information from its visa outlook database for the purpose of investigating or preventing crimes and to "deny visas to persons who would be inadmissable to the United States."
- Section 414 directs the Attorney General to fully implement an "integrated entry and exit data system for airports, seaports, and land border ports of entry," with a particular focus on the use of biometric technology and tamper-resistant documents.
- Section 701 authorizes the Office of Justice Programs to expand information sharing with state and local law enforcement agencies and nonprofit organizations to fight multi-jurisdictional criminal conspiracies. It also calls for the establishment of a secure information sharing system.
- Section 906 emphasizes the potential consolidation of data collection responsibilities by requiring the Attorney General, the Director of Central Intelligence, and the Secretary of the Treasury to submit a report to Congress "on the feasibility and desirability of reconfiguring the Foreign Terrorist Asset Tracking Center and the Office of Foreign Assets Control of the Department of Treasury in order to establish a capability to provide for the effective and efficient analysis and dissemination of foreign intelligence relating to the financial capabilities and resources of international terrorist organizations." The report is also to examine "to what extent the capabilities and resources of the Financial Crimes Enforcement Center of the Department of the Treasury may be integrated into the capability contemplated by the report."
- Section 1008 also focuses on the potential for data sharing between agencies. It calls for a study directed by the Attorney General in consultation with the Secretary of State and the Secretary of Transportation "on the feasibility of utilizing a biometric identifier (fingerprint) scanning system, with access to the database of the Federal Bureau of Investigation Integrated Automated Fingerprint Identification System, at consular offices abroad and at points of entry into the United States to enhance the ability of State

Department and immigration officials to identify aliens who may be wanted in connection with criminal or terrorist investigations in the United States or abroad prior to the issuance of visas or entry into the United States."

- Section 1009 focuses on potential information sharing between federal agencies and airlines. It directs the FBI to study "the feasibility of providing airlines access via computer to the names of passengers who are suspected of terrorist activity by federal officials."
- Section 1012 focuses on enhancing the cooperation between federal and state officials to limit the issuance of licenses to transport hazardous materials in commerce (hazmat licenses). It allows states to request the Attorney General to conduct a background check on applicants using "relevant international databases through Interpol" and other means.
- Section 1015 also focuses on intergovernmental relationships by expanding the scope and lengthening the authorization of appropriations of the Crime Identification Technology Act (P.L. 105-251), which allows the Office of Justice Programs to issue grants to state and local entities to develop integrated information and identification systems.

Policy Issues

The e-government policy implications associated with the USA PATRIOT Act are centered around three primary issues; knowledge management/data sharing, information security, and privacy.

Knowledge Management

Knowledge management (KM) has been defined as "the process through which an enterprise uses its collective intelligence to accomplish its strategic objectives."[28] As the above summary of the relevant provisions suggests, enhanced data sharing and knowledge management techniques are expected to play a significant role in homeland security efforts. Several of the provisions focus on improving access and the sharing of centralized databases by federal, state, and local law enforcement agencies. Some of the provisions also seek to establish a more fully integrated database system for

[28]Barquin, Ramon C., Alex Bennet, and Shereen G. Remez (eds.). *Knowledge Management: The Catalyst for Electronic Government*. Vienna, VA: Management Concepts, Inc., 2001, p. 5.

processing and tracking the granting of visas, as well as the entry and exit of foreign nationals in the United States. In many cases these provisions are designed to rectify the problems associated with having multiple, incompatible, and sometimes overlapping databases, which have been identified as one of the contributing factors to the difficulties law enforcement and intelligence agencies have had tracking suspected terrorists.[29] Just as knowledge management has been recognized as an important component of improved homeland security, its proponents argue that knowledge management could play a significant role in e-government initiatives generally. Knowledge management efforts involving e-government have so far encountered a variety of obstacles.[30] Some of these obstacles include creating the appropriate technical and support infrastructure, achieving user "buy-in," and managing the development and use of specialized information. Some have suggested the creation of the position of chief knowledge officers (CKOs) at the agency, department, and/or federal level to facilitate the execution of specific knowledge-intensive projects and support larger government reform efforts. The success of knowledge management/data sharing efforts in the homeland security area could affect the adoption of these proposals.

Ensuring Information Security

Heavy reliance on centralized databases with wider access by more actors (both governmental and non-governmental) will require careful attention to data protection and the authentication of users. One way this may be achieved is through the use of public key infrastructure (PKI) encryption systems.[31] PKI systems are generally considered the most reliable means to ensure the security of online transactions.[32] However, implementing a PKI system can be a very difficult, time consuming, and expensive process. Moreover, in the case of federal e-government projects, the PKI systems used by different departments and agencies would need to be interoperable in order to realize the efficiencies hoped for, and

---

[29] Porteus, Liza. FBI Official Laments Restrictions on Information Sharing. Government Executive Magazine, January 23, 2002. [http://www.govexec.com/dailyfed/0102/012302td1.htm].

[30] Caterinicchia, Dan. Cultural Changes Trumps Technology. Federal Computer Week, January 7, 2002, p. 21.

[31] A PKI is a system of digital certificates, certificate authorities, and other registration authorities that verify and authenticate the validity of each party involved in an Internet transaction. Certificate and registration authorities can be managed either by third party organizations or through in-house personnel.

[32] Robinson, Brian. PKI: A Necessary Evil. Federal Computer Week. September 3, 2001. [http://www.few.com/geb/articles/2001/sep/geb-tec2-09-01.asp].

convenience necessary, to achieve the desired citizen usage levels. So far, no such standards have been established.

The challenge of establishing a large scale PKI system raises many issues. Some of these include the lack of federal interoperable standards, the feasibility of implementation, and high costs.[33] First, the lack of federal interoperable standards raises the question of who would be responsible for developing and promulgating such standards. The National Institute of Standards and Technology (NIST) often works with industry to facilitate and develop technical standards and measurements. However, it is currently unclear what role NIST would play in developing any PKI standards. Assuming the acceptance of the PKI approach, it is also unclear whether the federal government should work to create a standard for its own use, or if it should rely on the development of an industry standard, which may take longer to emerge. Second, large scale, full-featured PKI systems are not common, raising questions regarding the scalability of the technology and the resources needed to accomplish the task. Implementation of such a system would require policy makers to decide if the federal government has sufficient expertise and resources to create a large scale PKI system in-house, or if it will need to be outsourced to one or more private contractors. Third, the largely uncharted nature of such an undertaking and the high costs of PKI systems generally, raises concerns for budget planning and oversight. Proponents of a government-wide PKI system maintain that if these issues can be adequately addressed, the creation of a single government-wide PKI system could promote the utilization of secure Web portals to ensure the data integrity of transactions between the government and citizens and business.

Privacy

In contrast to the two previously discussed issues, the implications of the USA PATRIOT Act on privacy could have a negative effect on e-government initiatives. Surveys have shown that the loss of privacy as a result of e-government is a significant concern among citizens.[34] As mentioned in the earlier section on computer security, the Act expands the type of information that may be collected by law enforcement officials from providers of electronic communications services or remote computing services. It also allows for the issuance of nationwide search warrants to facilitate the tracking of computer trespassers. Concerns about potential

[33]General Accounting Office, Information Security: Advances and Remaining Challenges to Adoption of Public Key Infrastructure Technology, GAO-01-277, February 2001, p.42.

[34]The Council for Excellence in Government. E-Government: The Next American Revolution, 2001, p. 27.

misuse of these data collection provisions could dampen citizen enthusiasm for carrying out electronic transactions with the government.

INTERNET PRIVACY: LAW ENFORCEMENT MONITORING OF INTERNET USAGE[35]

Until the September 11, 2001 terrorist acts, the Internet privacy debate focused on consumer privacy issues sparked by the collection, use, and dissemination of personally identifiable information by commercial Web site operators.[36] The practices of law enforcement agencies in monitoring the activities of individuals as they use the Internet for electronic mail (e-mail) or visiting Web sites was an important, but less visible, issue. Congress addressed it primarily in the context of ensuring that the Federal Bureau of Investigation (FBI) did not overstep its authority in using a software program called Carnivore (later renamed DCS 1000).[37] With a court order, the FBI could install Carnivore on the equipment of an Internet Service Provider (ISP) to monitor a suspect's Internet activity, which raised concern about whether the software was sufficiently precise to avoid monitoring the activity of other ISP customers and hence impinging on their privacy.

While Congress remains interested in overseeing the FBI's use of Carnivore, the September 11 terrorist attacks sharpened the debate over how to strike a balance between law enforcement's need to investigate criminals and protecting what most citizens believe to be their "right" to privacy.[38] Congress included provisions in the USA PATRIOT Act that make it easier for law enforcement to monitor Internet activities. Also, many ISPs that opposed law enforcement monitoring of their customers' Internet activity reportedly have been quite willing to assist law enforcement in its search for e-mail and other Internet evidence relating to the attacks.[39]

---

[35]Written by Marcia S. Smith, Specialist in Aerospace and Telecommunications Policy, CRS Resources, Science, and Industry Division.

[36]See CRS Report RL30784, *Internet Privacy: An Analysis of Technology and Policy Issues*, by Marcia S. Smith, for a discussion of those issues.

[37]For information on Congress' actions relative to Carnivore/DCS 1000, see CRS Report RS20035, *Internet Privacy: Overview and Pending Legislation*, by Marcia S. Smith.

[38]See CRS Report RL30671, *Personal Privacy Protection: The Legislative Response*, by Harold Relyea, for a discussion of the evolution of privacy rights in the United States.

[39]Matthews, William. Security Trumps Privacy in New Order. Federal Computer Week, September 24, 2001, p 40.

Provisions of the USA PATRIOT Act Affecting Internet Privacy

Title II of the Act, Enhanced Surveillance Procedures, includes provisions that affect monitoring of Internet activities.

- Section 210 expands the scope of subpoenas for records of electronic communications to include records commonly associated with Internet usage, such as session times and duration.
- Section 211 clarifies that cable companies offering Internet services are subject to 18 U.S.C. ch. 119 (Wire and Electronics Interception and Interception of Oral Communications), 18 U.S.C. ch. 121 (Stored Wire and Electronic Communications and Transactional Records Access), and 18 U.S.C. ch. 206 (Pen Registers and Trap and Trace Devices) in their provision of those services. Cable companies had sought, in particular, to clarify their obligations with regard to release of personally identifiable information about subscribers and whether they were required to notify the subscriber that the information had been requested by a governmental entity as required under the 1992 Cable Act. Under this section, no notification is required, but disclosure specifically does not include a subscriber's video programming choices.
- Section 212 *allows* ISPs to divulge records or other information (but not the contents of communications) pertaining to a subscriber if they believe there is immediate danger of death or serious physical injury or as otherwise authorized, and *requires* them to divulge such records or information (excluding contents of communications) to a governmental entity under certain conditions. It also allows an ISP to divulge the *contents* of communications to a law enforcement agency if it reasonably believes that an emergency involving immediate danger of death or serious physical injury requires disclosure of the information without delay.[40]
- Section 216 adds routing and addressing information (used in Internet communications) to dialing information, expanding what information a government agency may capture, as authorized by a

[40]Legislation (H.R. 3482) is currently pending before Congress that would amend this section of the USA PATRIOT Act to lower the threshold of the circumstances under which ISPs may divulge the contents of communications, and to whom they may divulge the contents. For information on current legislative status on that or other Internet privacy legislation, see CRS Report RS20035.

court order, using pen registers and trap and trace devices.[41] The content of any wire or electronic communications is excluded. A court shall enter an ex parte order permitting installation and use of a pen register or trap and trace device if it finds that an attorney for the government or a state law enforcement or investigative officer has certified that the information likely to be obtained is relevant to an ongoing criminal investigation. Law enforcement officials must keep certain records when they use their own pen registers or trap and trace devices and provide those records to the court that issued the order within 30 days of expiration of the order. To the extent that Carnivore-like systems fall with the new definition of pen registers or trap and trace devices provided in the Act, that language would increase judicial oversight of the use of such systems.

- Section 217 allows a person acting under color of law to intercept the wire or electronic communications of a computer trespasser transmitted to, through, or from a protected computer under certain circumstances.
- Section 220 allows for nationwide search warrants for e-mail instead of requiring separate search warrants for each jurisdiction in which the e-mail may be located, such as at the ISP's location rather than where a crime was committed.
- Section 224 establishes a 4-year sunset period (until December 31, 2005) for many of the Title II provisions, but among the sections excluded from the sunset are Sections 210, 211, and 216.

Policy Issues

As noted, the challenge for policy makers is balancing the needs of law enforcement with the desire by the public to maintain its privacy. In the wake of the terrorist attacks, the public appears more willing to make sacrifices in the privacy arena to protect the country against further attacks and bring the perpetrators of the September 11 assault to justice. Criticism of the USA PATRIOT Act from a privacy standpoint has been relatively muted, possibly because of the perception that the public is willing to accept such measures at this time. An October 2001 Harris Poll found that 63% of

[41] See footnote 6 for an explanation of pen registers and trap and trace devices.

Americans favored monitoring of Internet discussions and chat rooms, and 54% favored monitoring cell phones and e-mail.[42]

However, privacy advocates worry that, in this emotionally charged climate, Congress is passing legislation that it later will regret. Groups such as the American Civil Liberties Union (ACLU), Center for Democracy and Technology (CDT), Electronic Privacy Information Center (EPIC), and Electronic Frontier Foundation (EFF) urge caution, fearful that, in an attempt to track down and punish the terrorists who threaten American democracy, one of the fundamental tenets of that democracy—privacy—may itself be threatened. The ACLU issued a press release[43] on October 24 stating that it was deeply disappointed with the House passage of H.R. 3162, and, after the bill cleared Congress, vowed to monitor its implementation.[44] CDT's Executive Director said on October 25 that "This bill has been called a compromise but the only thing compromised is our civil liberties."[45] Among CDT's concerns is that Section 216, which is not subject to the sunset provision, allows law enforcement officials to collect information about Internet usage without what CDT considers to be meaningful judicial review.[46]

There are other privacy issues, too. Peter Swire, who served as privacy counselor at the Office of Management and Budget during the Clinton Administration, worries that the Act does not include sufficient provisions to deal with potential abuses by law enforcement of the new authorities granted in the Act.[47] Federal Trade Commission (FTC) Commissioner Orson Swindle has suggested that ISPs relook at their privacy policy statements in the wake of passage of the Act, particularly with regard to ISPs' new authority under Section 212 to voluntarily disclose information.[48] The FTC oversees how businesses, including ISPs, adhere to their privacy policies. Mr. Swindle also pointed out that it is his understanding that the law does not cover Web sites, only ISPs. He wondered if an online bookseller received many requests for books on, for example, how to make bombs or

---

[42]Schwartz, John. Seeking Privacy Online, Even as Security Tightens. New York Times, November 11, 2001, p. 10 Bu.

[43]ACLU press release October 26, 2001 [http://www.aclu.org/news/2001/n102401a.html].

[44]ACLU press release October 24, 2001 [http://www.aclu.org/news/2001/n102601a.html].

[45]CDT press release October 25, 2001 [http://www.cdt.org/press/011025press.shtml].

[46]CDT Policy Post 7.11, October 26, 2001. Available at [http://www.cdt.org].

[47]Swire, Peter. If Surveillance Expands, Safeguard Civil Liberties. Atlanta Journal-Constitution op-ed, October 21, 2001, p 2D. In its final form, the Act includes enhanced sanctions and other measures designed to reduce the risk of abuse, e.g., sections 223 (civil liability), 224 (sunset of some provisions), and 1001 (review of the Department of Justice).

[48]FTC's Swindle: PATRIOT Act May Require Updated ISP Privacy Policies. Communications Daily, November 30, 2001, p. 1-2.

fly an airplane, "and the name of the purchasers reflected one or another ethnic group, would that be alarming under concern for terrorism?... It would seem to me that common sense would say that would be alarming but they're not covered by this."[49] John Kamp, an attorney with Wiley, Rein & Fielding, commented that the definitions in the Act were murky and Web sites might be covered, but that "It is clear that this law wasn't designed to go there."[50]

The question of definitions is raised by others, including EFF. In particular, EFF cites the lack of definitions of "content" of e-mails that cannot be retrieved without a warrant, and the term "without authority" in the definition of a computer trespasser.[51] Packets of data that comprise e-mail messages may contain both content and non-content information (such as routing information). The Act allows law enforcement officials access to non-content information, but not to content. Thus this definition could be quite important. Regarding computer trespassers, Section 217 defines a computer trespasser as a person who accesses a protected computer without authorization, but it does not include a person with an existing contractual relationship with the owner or operator of the computer. EFF wants that term to mean only individuals who intentionally break into computers with which they have no relationship.

Some ISPs express satisfaction that guidance issued by the Justice Department implementing the USA PATRIOT Act clarifies that ISPs may use their own tools to obtain information required by law enforcement officials rather than rather than being required to allow the FBI to install software such as DCS 1000. EarthLink executive David Baker called it a "silver lining in what many otherwise describe as a cloud...."[52]

---

[49]Ibid.

[50]Ibid.

[51]EFF Analysis of the Provisions of the USA PATRIOT Act That Relate to Online Activities (Oct. 31, 2001). [http://www.eff.org/Privacy/Surveillance/Terrorism_militias/20011031_eff_usa_patriot_analysis.html]. The law does define "contents" and "electronic communications" for interception purposes, 18 U.S. C. 2518 (8), (12), although not for pen register or trap and trace device purposes, 18 USC.3127.

[52]Communications Daily, November 30, 2001, op cit.

Like the ACLU, most of the privacy advocate groups assert that they will closely monitor how law enforcement officials implement the Act and try to ensure that the law is not misused. Congress may conduct oversight of the Act's implementation, both from the standpoint of the value of providing law enforcement officials with these additional tools to combat crime and terrorism, and in terms of any detrimental consequences that could arise.

Chapter 3

THE USA PATRIOT ACT: A SKETCH

Charles Doyle

SUMMARY

Congress passed the USA PATRIOT Act (the Act) in response to the terrorists' attacks of September 11, 2001. The Act gives federal officials greater authority to track and intercept communications, both for law enforcement and foreign intelligence gathering purposes. It vests the Secretary of the Treasury with regulatory powers to combat corruption of U.S. financial institutions for foreign money laundering purposes. It seeks to further close our borders to foreign terrorists and to detain and remove those within our borders. It creates new crimes, new penalties, and new procedural efficiencies for use against domestic and international terrorists. Although it is not without safeguards, critics contend some of its provisions go too far. Although it grants many of the enhancements sought by the Department of Justice, others are concerned that it does not go far enough.

The Act originated as H.R.2975 (the PATRIOT Act) in the House and S.1510 in the Senate (the USA Act), S.1510 passed the Senate on October 11, 2001, 147 *Cong.Rec.* S10604 (daily ed.). The House Judiciary Committee reported out an amended version of H.R. 2975 on the same day. H.R.Rep No. 107-236. The House passed H.R. 2975 the following day after substituting the text of H.R. 3108, 147 *Cong.Rec.* H6775-776 (daily ed. Oct. 12, 2001). The House version incorporated most of the money laundering provisions found in an earlier House bill, H.R. 3004, many of which had counterparts in S.1510 as approved by the Senate. The House subsequently passed a clean bill, H.R. 3162 (under suspension of the rules), which resolved the differences between H.R. 2975 and S.1510, 147 *Cong.Rec.* H7224 (daily ed. Oct. 24, 2001). The Senate agreed to the changes, 147 *Cong.Rec.* S10969 (daily ed. Oct. 24, 2001), and H.R. 3162 was sent to the President who signed it on October 26, 2001.

Criminal Investigations: Tracking and Gathering Communications

Federal communications privacy law features a three tiered system, erected for the dual purpose of protecting the confidentiality of private telephone, face-to-face, and computer communications while enabling authorities to identify and intercept criminal communications. Title III of the Omnibus Crime Control and Safe Streets Act of 1968 supplies the first level. It prohibits electronic eavesdropping on telephone conversations, face-to-face conversations, or computer and other forms of electronic communications in most instances. It does, however, give authorities a narrowly defined process for electronic surveillance to be used as a last resort in serious criminal cases. When approved by senior Justice Department officials, law enforcement officers may seek a court order authorizing them to secretly capture conversations concerning any of a statutory list of offenses (predicate offenses). Title III court orders come replete with instructions describing the permissible duration and scope of the surveillance as well as the conversations which may be seized and the efforts to be taken to minimize the seizure of innocent conversations. The court notifies the parties to any conversations seized under the order after the order expires.

Below Title III, the next tier of privacy protection covers telephone records, e-mail held in third party storage, and the like, 18 U.S.C. 2701-2709 (Chapter 121). Here, the law permits law enforcement access, ordinarily pursuant to a warrant or court order or under a subpoena in some cases, but in connection with *any* criminal investigation and without the extraordinary levels of approval or constraint that mark a Title III interception.

Least demanding and perhaps least intrusive of all is the procedure that governs court orders approving the government's use of trap and trace devices and pen registers, a kind of secret "caller id.", which identify the source and destination of calls made to and from a particular telephone, 18 U.S.C. 3121-3127 (Chapter 206). The orders are available based on the government's certification, rather than a finding of a court, that use of the device is likely to produce information relevant to the investigation of a crime, any crime. The devices record no more than identity of the participants in a telephone conversation, but neither the orders nor the results they produce need ever be revealed to the participants.

The Act modifies the procedures at each of the three levels. It:

- permits pen register and trap and trace orders for electronic communications (*e.g.*, e-mail);
- authorizes nationwide execution of court orders for pen registers, trap and trace devices, and access to stored e-mail or communication records;
- treats stored voice mail like stored e-mail (rather than like telephone conversations);
- permits authorities to intercept communications to and from a trespasser within a computer system (with the permission of the system's owner);
- adds terrorist and computer crimes to Title III's predicate offense list;
- reenforces protection for those who help execute Title III, ch. 121, and ch. 206 orders;
- encourages cooperation between law enforcement and foreign intelligence investigators;
- establishes a claim against the U.S. for certain communications privacy violations by government personnel; and
- terminates the authority found in many of these provisions and several of the foreign intelligence amendments with a sunset provision (Dec. 31, 2005).

FOREIGN INTELLIGENCE INVESTIGATIONS

The Act eases some of the restrictions on foreign intelligence gathering within the United States, and affords the U.S. intelligence community greater access to information unearthed during a criminal investigation, but it also establishes and expands safeguards against official abuse. More specifically, it:

- permits "roving" surveillance (court orders omitting the identification of the particular instrument, facilities, or place where the surveillance is to occur when the court finds the target is likely to thwart identification with particularity);
- increases the number of judges on the Foreign Intelligence Surveillance Act (FISA) court from 7 to 11;
- allows application for a FISA surveillance or search order when gathering foreign intelligence is *a significant* reason for the application rather than *the* reason;
- authorizes pen register and trap & trace device orders for e-mail as well as telephone conversations;
- sanctions court ordered access to any tangible item rather than only business records held by lodging, car rental, and locker rental businesses;
- carries a sunset provision;
- establishes a claim against the U.S. for certain communications privacy violations by government personnel; and
- expands the prohibition against FISA orders based solely on an American's exercise of his or her First Amendment rights.

MONEY LAUNDERING

In federal law, money laundering is the flow of cash or other valuables derived from, or intended to facilitate, the commission of a criminal offense. It is the movement of the fruits and instruments of crime. Federal authorities attack money laundering through regulations, criminal sanctions, and forfeiture. The Act bolsters federal efforts in each area.

Regulation

The Act expands the authority of the Secretary of the Treasury to regulate the activities of U.S. financial institutions, particularly their relations with foreign individuals and entities. He is to promulgate regulations:

- under which securities brokers and dealers as well as commodity merchants, advisors and pool operators must file suspicious activity reports (SARs);

- requiring businesses, which were only to report cash transactions involving more than $10,000 to the IRS, to file SARs as well;
- imposing additional "special measures" and "due diligence" requirements to combat foreign money laundering;
- prohibiting U.S. financial institutions from maintaining correspondent accounts for foreign shell banks;
- preventing financial institutions from allowing their customers to conceal their financial activities by taking advantage of the institutions' concentration account practices;
- establishing minimum new customer identification standards and record-keeping and recommending an effective means to verify the identity of foreign customers;
- encouraging financial institutions and law enforcement agencies to share information concerning suspected money laundering and terrorist activities; and
- requiring financial institutions to maintain anti-money laundering programs which must include at least a compliance officer; an employee training program; the development of internal policies, procedures and controls; and an independent audit feature.

Crimes

The Act contains a number of new money laundering crimes, as well as amendments and increased penalties for earlier crimes. It:

- outlaws laundering (in the U.S.) any of the proceeds from foreign crimes of violence or political corruption;
- prohibits laundering the proceeds from cybercrime or supporting a terrorist organization;
- increases the penalties for counterfeiting;
- seeks to overcome a Supreme Court decision finding that the confiscation of over $300,000 (for attempt to leave the country without reporting it to customs) constituted an unconstitutionally excessive fine;
- provides explicit authority to prosecute overseas fraud involving American credit cards; and
- endeavors to permit prosecution of money laundering in the place where the predicate offense occurs.

Forfeiture

The Act creates two types of forfeitures and modifies several confiscation-related procedures. It allows confiscation of all of the property of any individual or entity that participates in or plans an act of domestic or international terrorism; it also permits confiscation of any property derived from or used to facilitate domestic or international terrorism. The Constitution's due process, double jeopardy, and ex post facto clauses may limit the anticipated breath of these provisions. Procedurally, the Act:

- establishes a mechanism to acquire long arm jurisdiction, for purposes of forfeiture proceedings, over individuals and entities;
- allows confiscation of property located in this country for a wider range of crimes committed in violation of foreign law;
- permits U.S. enforcement of foreign forfeiture orders;
- calls for the seizure of correspondent accounts held in U.S. financial institutions for foreign banks who are in turn holding forfeitable assets overseas; and
- denies corporate entities the right to contest a confiscation if their principal shareholder is a fugitive.

Alien Terrorists and Victims

The Act contains a number of provisions designed to prevent alien terrorists from entering the United States, particularly from Canada; to enable authorities to detain and deport alien terrorists and those who support them; and to provide humanitarian immigration relief for foreign victims of the attacks on September 11.

Other Crimes, Penalties, & Procedures

New Crimes

The Act creates new federal crimes for terrorist attacks on mass transportation facilities, for biological weapons offenses, for harboring terrorists, for affording terrorists material support, for misconduct associated with money laundering already mentioned, for conducting the affairs of an enterprise which affects interstate or foreign commerce through the patterned commission of terrorist offenses, and for fraudulent charitable solicitation. Although strictly speaking these are new federal crimes, they generally supplement existing law by filling gaps and increasing penalties.

New Penalties

The Act increases the penalties for acts of terrorism and for crimes which terrorists might commit. More specifically it establishes an alternative maximum penalty for acts of terrorism, raises the penalties for conspiracy to commit certain terrorist offenses, envisions sentencing some terrorists to life-long parole, and increases the penalties for counterfeiting, cybercrime, and charity fraud.

Other Procedural Adjustments

In other procedural adjustments designed to facilitate criminal investigations, the Act:

- increases the rewards for information in terrorism cases;
- expands the Posse Comitatus Act exceptions;
- authorizes "sneak and peek" search warrants;
- permits nationwide and perhaps worldwide execution of warrants in terrorism cases;
- eases government access to confidential information;
- allows the Attorney General to collect DNA samples from prisoners convicted of any federal crime of violence or terrorism;
- lengthens the statute of limitations applicable to crimes of terrorism;
- clarifies the application of federal criminal law on American installations and in residences of U.S. government personnel overseas; and
- adjust federal victims' compensation and assistance programs.

A section, found in the Senate bill but ultimately dropped, would have changed the provision of federal law which requires Justice Department prosecutors to adhere to the ethical standards of the legal profession where they conduct their activities (the McDade-Murtha Amendment), 28 U.S.C. 530B.

INDEX

D

N

O

P

R

S

T

U

V

W